JOB EVALUATION

A Guide To Achieving Equal Pay

Michael Armstrong
Ann Cummins
Sue Hastings
Willie Wood

WITHDRAWN

KOGAN PAGE

First published in Great Britain and the United States in 2003 by Kogan Page Limited
Paperback edition 2005
Reprinted 2007 (twice)

120 Pentonville Road
London N1 9JN
UK

525 South 4th Street #241
Philadelphia PA 19147
USA

www.kogan-page.co.uk

ISBN-10 0 7494 4481 9
ISBN-13 978 0 7494 4481 5

British Library Cataloguing in Publication Data

A CIP record for this book is available from the British Library.

Library of Congress Cataloging-in-Publication Data

Job evaluation : a guide to achieving equal pay / Michael Armstrong ... [et al.].
    p. cm
Includes bibliographical references and index.
    ISBN 0-7497-3966-1
    1. Job evaluation. 2. Job evaluation–Great Britain. I. Armstrong, Michael, 1928–
    HF5549.5.J62J634 2003
    6758.3'06--dc22
                                        2003016407

Typeset by Saxon Graphics Ltd, Derby
Printed and bound in Great Britain by Biddles Ltd, King's Lynn
www.biddles.co.uk

Contents

Introduction

The aim of this book is to provide a guide to good practice in the design, development and use of job evaluation schemes with particular reference to equal pay considerations. It makes extensive use of the practical experience of its authors in job evaluation, especially in dealing with equal pay issues.

A special survey conducted by E-Reward in late 2002 provided valuable information on what is happening currently to job evaluation in the UK. One of the most important findings of this survey is that interest in job evaluation is growing – it is not declining, as many people believed in the 1990s. The recent national focus on equal pay matters has contributed to its greater popularity but in the experience of the writers of this book, as confirmed by the survey, many organizations increasingly believe that job evaluation is an essential tool for the development and management of a logical and defensible grade and pay structure as part of an overarching reward strategy.

The book starts with a review of the basic features of job evaluation and a summary of the survey findings. It then deals with equal value considerations and the conduct of equal pay reviews. The next four chapters contain guidance on the planning and design of job evaluation schemes, the use of computers and the design of grade and pay structures. The book ends with guidelines on the introduction and management of job evaluation.

1

Fundamentals of job evaluation

In this introductory chapter:

▮ job evaluation is defined;

▮ the purpose, aims and features of job evaluation are explained;

▮ the extent to which job evaluation is used is described;

▮ the arguments for and against job evaluation are summarized;

▮ conclusions are reached about the future of job evaluation.

The main types of job evaluation schemes are described in Chapter 2.

JOB EVALUATION DEFINED

Job evaluation is a systematic process for defining the relative worth or size of jobs within an organization in order to establish internal relativities and provide the basis for designing an equitable grade and pay structure, grading jobs in the structure and managing relativities. Job evaluation can be analytical or non-analytical.

Analytical job evaluation schemes

These are schemes in which decisions about the value or size of jobs are based on an analysis of the extent to which various defined factors or elements are present in a job. These factors should be present in all the jobs to be evaluated and the different levels at which they are present indicate relative job value. The Equal Pay (Amendment) Regulations (1983) refer to 'the demands on a worker under various headings, for instance, effort, skill, decision'.

The most common analytical approach is a points-factor scheme where there is a 'factor plan' which defines the factors and their levels and attaches scores to each level. Following job analysis, scores for each factor are awarded and then totalled. On completion of an evaluation programme, the total scores for jobs indicate their rank order. This type of scheme can meet the requirements of equal value law as long as it is not in itself discriminatory either in its design or application. To ensure that equity considerations are catered for in an organization, it is preferable to use only one scheme which must therefore be designed to cover the key features of each category of job at every level.

Non-analytical job evaluation schemes

These are schemes in which whole jobs are described and compared in order to place them in rank order or in a grade without analysing them into their constituent parts or elements. The most common non-analytical approach is to 'match' roles as defined in role profiles to definitions of grades or bands (this is often referred to as job classification), or to the role profiles of jobs that have already been graded. When designing grade structures, however, the initial step may be to rank the jobs in order of perceived value (job ranking). Non-analytical schemes do not meet the requirements of equal value law.

PURPOSE, AIMS AND FEATURES OF JOB EVALUATION

Purpose

Job evaluation, especially analytical job evaluation, enables a framework to be designed which underpins grading and therefore pay decisions. It is particularly important as a means of achieving equal pay for work of equal value. In its *Good Practice Guide – Job Evaluation Schemes Free of Sex Bias*, the Equal Opportunities Commission (EOC) emphasizes that: 'Non-discriminatory job evaluation should lead to a payment system which is transparent and within which work of equal value receives equal pay regardless of sex.' This statement only refers to equal pay 'regardless of sex' but job evaluation is just as concerned with achieving equal pay regardless of race or disability or indeed age.

Aims of job evaluation

Job evaluation aims to:

- establish the relative value or size of jobs, ie internal relativities;

- produce the information required to design and maintain equitable and defensible grade and pay structures;

- provide as objective as possible a basis for grading jobs within a grade structure, thus enabling consistent decisions to be made about job grading;

- ensure that the organization meets ethical and legal equal pay for work of equal value obligations.

The last aim is important – analytical job evaluation plays a crucial part in achieving equal pay for work of equal value. It is an essential ingredient in equal pay reviews or audits, as described in Chapter 5.

Features of analytical job evaluation

To meet fundamental equal pay for work of equal value requirements, job evaluation schemes must be analytical. Non-analytical 'job matching' methods may be used to allocate or 'slot' jobs into grades but these have to be underpinned by an analytical scheme. The main features of analytical job evaluation, as explained below, are that it is systematic, judgemental, concerned with the person not the job, and deals with internal relativities.

Systematic

Job evaluation is systematic in that the relative value or 'size' of jobs is determined on the basis of factual evidence on the characteristics of the jobs which has been analysed within a structured framework of criteria or factors.

Judgemental

Although job evaluations are based on factual evidence, this has to be interpreted. The information provided about jobs through job analysis can sometimes fail to provide a clear indication of the levels at which demands are present in a job. The definitions in the factor plan may not precisely indicate the level of demand that should be recorded. Judgement is required in making decisions on the level and therefore, in a points-factor scheme, the score. The aim is to maximize objectivity but it is difficult to eliminate a degree of subjectivity. As the Equal Opportunities Commission (EOC) states in its *Good Practice Guide – Job Evaluation Schemes Free of Sex Bias:* 'it is recognised that to a certain extent any assessment of a job's total demands relative to another will always be subjective'. A fundamental aim of any process of job evaluation is to ensure that, as far as possible, consistent judgements are made based on objectively assessed information.

Concerned with the job not the person

This is the iron law of job evaluation. It means that when evaluating a job the only concern is the content of that job in terms of the demands made on the jobholder. The performance of the individual in the job must not be taken into account. But it should be noted that while _performance_ is excluded, in today's more flexible organizations the tendency is for some people, especially knowledge workers, to have flexible roles. Individuals may have the scope to enlarge or enrich their roles and this needs to be taken into account when evaluating what they do, as long as this is appropriate within the context of their basic role. Roles cannot necessarily be separated from the people who carry them out. It is people who create value, not jobs.

It is necessary to distinguish between the concept of a job and that of a role.

A _job_ consists of a group of finite tasks to be performed (pieces of work) and duties to be fulfilled in order to achieve an end-result. Job descriptions basically list a number of tasks.

A _role_ describes the part played by people in carrying out their work by working competently and flexibly within the context of the organization's culture, structure and processes. Role profiles set out the behavioural requirements of the role as well as the outcomes expected of those who perform it.

Concerned with internal relativities

When used within an organization, job evaluation can only assess the relative size of jobs in that organization. It is not concerned with external relativities, that is, the relationship between the rates of pay of jobs in the organization and the rates of pay of comparable jobs elsewhere (market rates).

THE INCIDENCE OF JOB EVALUATION

An analysis of the responses of 316 organizations to a survey carried out by the Institute of Personnel and Development in 1994 established that 55 per cent of the respondents operated a formal job evaluation scheme. Of these, 68 per cent used a consultant's package (a 'proprietary brand' scheme). By far the most popular proprietary scheme (78 per cent of users) was the Hay Management Consultants Guide Chart Method. Of those respondents not using a proprietary brand, the most common method (29 per cent) was points-factor rating.

The most recent survey was conducted by E-Reward research in late 2002 (summarized in Chapter 3). It found that 44 per cent of the 236 organizations contributing to the research had a formal job evaluation scheme, and 45 per cent of those who did not have such a scheme intended to introduce one. This is in line with the findings of the reward survey conducted by the CIPD in 2002 which established that just over 42 per cent of respondents had job evaluation for managers and non-manual jobholders.

THE CASE FOR AND AGAINST JOB EVALUATION

The case for

The case for properly devised and applied job evaluation, especially analytical job evaluation, is that:

- it can make the criteria against which jobs are valued explicit and provide a basis for structuring the judgement process;

- an equitable and defensible pay structure cannot be achieved unless a structured and systematic process is used to assess job values and relativities;

- a logical framework is required within which consistent decisions can be made on job grades and rates of pay;

- analytical schemes provide the best basis for achieving equal pay for work of equal value and are the only acceptable defence in an equal pay case;

- a formal process of job evaluation is more likely to be accepted as fair and equitable than informal or ad hoc approaches – and the degree of acceptability will be considerably enhanced if the whole process is transparent.

The case against

The case against job evaluation has been presented vociferously. Critics emphasize that it can be bureaucratic, inflexible, time consuming and inappropriate in today's organizations. Schemes can decay over time through use or misuse. People learn how to manipulate them to achieve a higher grade and this leads to the phenomenon known as grade drift – upgradings which are not justified by a sufficiently significant increase in responsibility. Job evaluators can fall into the trap of making *a priori* judgements. They may judge the validity of a job evaluation exercise according to the extent to which it corresponds with their preconceptions about relative worth. The so-called 'felt-fair' test is used to assess the acceptability of job evaluations, but a rank order is felt to be fair if it reproduces their notion of what it ought to be.

These criticisms focus on the way in which job evaluation is operated rather than the concept of job evaluation itself. Like any other management technique, job evaluation schemes can be misconceived and misused and a prime aim of this book is to indicate how these pitfalls can be avoided. Indeed, the hostility to job evaluation prevalent in the 1980s has been significantly reduced recently by the general acceptance of the importance of achieving equity through a systematic approach to valuing jobs coupled with the increased focus on equal pay and the recognition that analytical job evaluation is an essential element in achieving equality. It is these beliefs that have encouraged the recent development of new job evaluation schemes by organizations and sectors such as the National Health Service, local government, higher education and further education.

CONCLUSIONS

It could be claimed that every time a decision is made on what a job should be paid requires a form of job evaluation. Job evaluation is therefore unavoidable but it should not be an intuitive, subjective and potentially biased process. The issue is how best to carry it out analytically, fairly, systematically, consistently, transparently and, so far as possible, objectively, without being bureaucratic, inflexible or resource intensive. There are four ways of dealing with this issue:

1. Use a tested and relevant analytical job evaluation scheme to inform and support the processes of designing grade structures, grading jobs, managing relativities and ensuring that work of equal value is paid equally.

2. Computerize job evaluation to a greater or lesser degree, as described in Chapter 8. The aim is to speed up processing and decision making while at the same time generating more consistent evaluations and reducing bureaucracy.

3. Recognize that thorough training and continuing guidance for evaluators are essential.

4. Review the operation of the scheme regularly to ensure that it is not decaying and continues to be appropriate.

The future of job evaluation

The E-Reward survey of job evaluation schemes summarized in Chapter 3 indicated that interest in job evaluation is increasing generally. Many organizations besides those mentioned above are continuing to develop and maintain their job evaluation schemes, although they may be used in a supporting rather than a driving role. This means relying on analytical job evaluation for help in designing grade structures, dealing with new or significantly changed jobs and informing equal pay reviews. But on a day-to-day basis, job evaluation may not be invoked to grade jobs unless they are special cases. Grading decisions may be made by 'matching' role profiles with level definitions. But job evaluation can always be brought to the fore when needed, especially to review or investigate equal pay matters.

These approaches are helping to ensure that job evaluation is here to stay. But it still requires a lot of effort to make it work well, as will be explained in later chapters in this book.

2

Types of job evaluation

The main types of job evaluation are described in this chapter as follows:

▋ *analytical schemes*: points-factor rating and factor comparison;

▋ *non-analytical schemes*: job ranking, paired comparison ranking and job classification;

▋ *non-analytical approaches (methods of grading or valuing jobs which are not schemes in the sense of those listed above, although they may be used in conjunction with such schemes)*: job matching and market pricing.

The chapter concludes with notes on design and process criteria and the criteria for choice.

ANALYTICAL SCHEMES

Points-factor rating

Points-factor rating is an analytical method of job evaluation which is based on breaking down jobs into factors or key elements. It is assumed that each of the factors will contribute to job size and is an aspect of all the jobs to be evaluated but to different degrees. Using numerical scales, points are allocated to a job under each factor heading according to the extent to which it is present in the job. The separate factor scores are then added together to give a total score which represents job size. The methodology used in points-factor schemes is described below.

1. Factor selection

A number of job factors are selected or defined (usually at least four or five and often twelve or more). These are characteristics of jobs which express the demands made on jobholders in such areas as decision making, the exercise of interpersonal skills, responsibility for people and other financial or non-financial resources, emotional demands and physical demands; the inputs required from jobholders in the form of knowledge, skills and competences and, sometimes, the outputs expected in the form of impact on results. Job evaluation factors break down the key components of jobs and the set of factors as a whole represent each of the most important elements of those jobs. The different levels at which individual factors apply to jobs provide information which indicates, when considered collectively, relative job value or size.

Care has to be taken when selecting factors to ensure that they do not discriminate in favour of either sex or any racial group. It is also necessary to avoid double counting (undue repetition of job characteristics in different factors).

2. Factor plan design

The factor plan consists of the factors themselves, each of which is divided into a number of levels. The number of levels depends on the range of demands or degrees of responsibility in a particular factor which might be present in the jobs to be covered by the scheme. The number could be as few as three or as many as eight. Typically, the number tends to be between five and seven.

The levels in each factor are defined to provide guidance on deciding the degree to which they apply in a job to be evaluated. The decision on levels is made by reference to an analysis of the job in terms of the factors.

A maximum points score is allocated to each factor. The scores may vary between different factors in accordance with beliefs about their relative significance. This is termed explicit weighting. If the number of levels varies between factors, this means that they are implicitly weighted.

The total score for a factor is divided between the levels to produce the factor scale. Progression may be arithmetic, eg 50, 100, 150, 200 etc, or geometric, eg 50, 100, 175, 275 etc. In the latter case, more scope is given to recognize the more senior jobs with higher scores.

3. Job or role analysis

Jobs or roles are analysed systematically in terms of each of the factors. The aim is to provide factual and explicit evidence which in a conventional non-computerized job evaluation scheme will guide evaluators in selecting the level at which the factor exists in a job. The job or role analysis may be based on a paper questionnaire completed by the jobholder and, usually, checked by the jobholder's line manager. Alternatively, information about a job may be input direct to a PC without the need to prepare a separate paper questionnaire.

4. Evaluating jobs

In a non-computerized scheme, jobs are usually evaluated by a panel which may, indeed should, include staff or union representatives as well as line managers and one or more members of the HR department. The panel studies the job analysis and agrees on the level and therefore the score that should be allocated for each factor and, ultimately, the total score.

In conventional computer-assisted schemes, as described in Chapter 8, the job analysis data is either entered direct into the computer or transferred to it from a paper questionnaire. The computer software applies pre-determined rules to convert the data into scores for each factor and produce a total score.

In an interactive computer-assisted scheme, as also described in Chapter 8, the jobholder and his or her manager sit in front of a PC and are presented with a series of logically interrelated questions, the answers to which lead to a score for each of the built-in factors in turn and a total score.

Whichever approach is adopted, it may be decided when introducing job evaluation to evaluate initially a representative sample of jobs – 'benchmark jobs' – as a basis for developing a grade structure.

5. Grading jobs

When a job evaluation exercise is being conducted to inform the design or revision of a graded pay structure the outcome will be a rank order of jobs according to their total scores. This rank order is then divided into grades, each of which is defined in terms of a bracket of job evaluation points. Pay ranges are then attached to each grade which will take account of external relativities (market rates). There is no direct relationship between job evaluation points and rates of pay – 'points don't mean pounds'. The points in a job evaluation scheme have no value in themselves. They are simply ordinal numbers which define the position of an entity in a series. All jobs within a grade will be paid within the same range of pay irrespective of their individual job evaluation scores (they are assumed to be of equal value) and pay ranges attached to grades may vary even when the job evaluation points ranges are the same.

The grading process may initially be based on the benchmark jobs. Other distinct jobs may then be evaluated and graded. This may not be necessary where there are any generic roles (ie those with basically the same range and level of responsibilities) and it is certain that the characteristics of a particular role or group of roles are virtually identical to these generic roles. In these circumstances the grading may be accomplished by matching the role to be graded with an appropriate generic role.

Once a graded pay structure has been designed, the points-factor job evaluation scheme can be used to determine where new or changed roles should be fitted into the structure. It can be invoked when individuals or managers believe that a job should be upgraded. However, as noted at the end of Chapter 1, some organizations are not using their job evaluation scheme as a matter of course and instead 'match' jobs to those that have already been graded where such comparisons can reasonably be made.

6. Reviews and appeals

The scheme should provide for a regular formal review of evaluations to ensure that they are valid and consistent. Employees should be allowed to appeal against an evaluation.

Advantages and disadvantages of points-factor rating

The advantages of points-factor schemes are that:

▪ evaluators have to consider a number of defined factors which, as long as they are present in all the jobs and affect them in different ways, reduce the risk of the over-simplified judgements that can be made when using non-analytical schemes;

▪ they provide evaluators with defined yardsticks which should help them to achieve a reasonable degree of objectivity and consistency in making their judgements;

▪ they at least *appear* to be objective and thus encourage people to believe that they are fair;

▪ they provide a rationale which helps in the design of graded pay structures;

▪ they adapt well to computerization;

▪ last but by no means least, they facilitate the achievement of equal pay for work of equal value and provide a defence in an equal value case as long as they are not discriminatory in themselves.

The disadvantages of points-factor schemes are that:

▪ it is still necessary to use judgement in selecting factors, defining levels in factors, deciding on weightings (if any), and interpreting information about jobs by reference to the definitions of factors and factor levels;

▌ they give a somewhat spurious impression of scientific accuracy – attaching points to subjective judgements does not make them any more objective;

▌ they assume that it is possible to quantify different aspects of jobs on the same scale of values; but job characteristics cannot necessarily be added together in this way.

However, the advantages of an analytical approach far outweigh these disadvantages. It may not guarantee total objectivity and, ultimately, it may do no more than give guidance on where jobs should be placed in a graded pay structure in relation to other jobs – the process of grading jobs is essentially judgemental. But it does provide the only acceptable method of dealing with equal pay issues and the judgements made are at least based on systematically collected and analysed evidence rather than dubious assumptions about relativities.

Factor comparison

The original and now little-used factor comparison method compared jobs factor by factor using a scale of money values to provide a direct indication of the rate for the job. The two forms of factor comparison now in use are graduated factor comparison and analytical factor comparison.

Graduated factor comparison

Graduated factor comparison involves comparing jobs factor by factor with a graduated scale. The scale may have only three value levels – for example lower, equal, higher – and no factor scores are used.

It is a method often used by the independent experts engaged by Employment Tribunals to advise on an equal pay claim. Their job is simply to compare one job with one or two others, not to review internal relativities over the whole spectrum of jobs in order to produce a rank order. Independent experts may score their judgements of comparative levels, in which case graduated factor comparison resembles the points-factor method except that the number of levels and range of scores are limited, and the factors may not be weighted.

Graduated factor comparison can be used within organizations if there is a problem of comparable worth and no other analytical scheme is available. It can also be used in a benchmarking exercise to assess relativities across different categories of employees in the absence of a common analytical job evaluation scheme as long as the factors used are common to all the job categories under consideration.

Analytical factor comparison

Analytical factor comparison is also based on the analysis of a number of defined factors. Role analysis takes place to assess the extent to which each of these factors or characteristics are present in a role and this analysis is recorded in the form of a role profile. Comparisons can then be made factor by factor between roles but no scale is used. Analytical factor comparison can also be used to grade roles by comparing the role profiles with grade definitions expressed under the same factor headings. This is a form of job classification, as described later in this chapter, but with an analytical element.

In theory, analytical factor comparison could be used to produce a rank order by the process of paired comparisons (as described later). In practice, however, this is an elaborate and time-consuming procedure and is seldom used.

Advantages and disadvantages of factor comparison

The advantages of factor comparison are that:

▓ it is analytical in the sense that it compares roles to roles or roles to grade definitions on a factor-by factor basis;

▓ as an analytical scheme it can, if non-discriminatory in design or application, be used to deal with equal pay issues and provide a defence in an equal pay case (case law only requires that the scheme should be analytical, not that it should be a points-factor method);

▓ it avoids what some people believe to be the artificial precision of points-factor rating;

▌ it can be used in benchmarking exercises – comparing roles in different job categories or families where there is no common system of analytical evaluation.

The disadvantages of factor comparison are that:

▌ evaluators are not provided with defined yardsticks in the shape of level definitions to aid the judgement process;

▌ it can therefore appear to be more subjective and prone to bias than a points-factor scheme;

▌ it cannot be used to rank jobs (unless a tedious process of paired comparisons is used);

▌ in practice its analytical nature is more apparent than real – the natural tendency is still to make whole-job comparisons by reference to assumptions about where a job should be graded which can too easily override the analytical data.

These disadvantages appear to convince most people that points-factor analytical schemes are preferable within organizations, although there may be situations where factor comparison can be used for direct comparisons of roles and for benchmarking.

NON-ANALYTICAL SCHEMES

The five main non-analytical schemes as described below are job ranking, paired comparison (a statistical form of job ranking), job classification, job matching and market pricing. Strictly speaking, the latter two are approaches to grading or valuing rather than conventional job evaluation schemes.

Job ranking

Ranking is the process of comparing whole jobs with one another and arranging them in order of their size or value to the organization. In a sense, all evaluation schemes are ranking exercises because they place jobs in a hierarchy. The difference between ranking and analytical methods such as points-factor rating is that job ranking does not attempt to quantify judgements. Instead, whole jobs are compared – they are not broken down into factors or elements, although, explicitly or implicitly, the comparison may be based on some generalized concept such as the level of responsibility.

Ranking may simply involve first identifying the jobs which are perceived to be the ones with the highest and lowest value, then selecting a job midway between the two, and finally choosing others at lower or higher intermediate points. The remainder of the jobs under review are then grouped around the key jobs, with ranking carried out within each sub-group. This achieves a complete ranking of all the jobs, which should be subjected to careful scrutiny to identify any jobs that appear to be 'out of line' – wrongly placed in the rank order.

Alternatively, ranking may be carried out by identifying and placing in order a number of clearly differentiated and well-defined benchmark jobs at various levels. The other jobs are ranked by comparing them with the benchmarks and slotting them in at an appropriate point.

The advantages of job ranking are that it is simple and easily understood and quick and cheap to implement, as long as agreement can be reached on the rank order of the jobs without too much argument. But:

▋ the process of comparing whole jobs means that there is no analytical framework to ensure that proper consideration is given to each of the key characteristics of the jobs being ranked;

▋ there are no defined standards for judging relative size or value, which means that there is no rationale to explain or defend the rank order;

▋ ranking is not acceptable as a method of determining comparable worth in equal value cases;

▋ evaluators need an overall knowledge of every job to be evaluated and ranking may be more difficult when a large number of jobs are under consideration;

▌ it may be difficult, if not impossible, to rank jobs in widely different functions where the demands made upon them vary significantly;

▌ it may be hard to justify slotting new jobs into the structure or to decide whether or not there is a case for moving a job up the rank order, ie regrading.

Ranking may be an easy method of job evaluation but its disadvantages far outweigh its advantages. The most telling point against it is that it cannot be used to deal with equal pay for work of equal value issues and it is not acceptable as a defence in an equal pay case.

Paired comparison ranking

Paired comparison ranking is a statistical technique which is used to provide a more sophisticated method of whole-job ranking. It is based on the assumption that it is always easier to compare one job with another than to consider a number of jobs and attempt to build up a rank order by multiple comparisons.

The technique requires the comparison of each job as a whole separately with every other job. If a job is considered to be of a higher value than the one with which it is being compared, it receives two points; if it is thought to be equally important, it receives one point; if it is regarded as less important, no points are awarded. The scores are added for each job and a rank order is obtained.

A simplified version of a paired comparison ranking form is shown in Figure 2.1.

Job reference	a	b	c	d	e	f	Total score	Ranking
A	–	0	1	0	1	0	2	5=
B	2	–	2	2	2	0	8	2
C	1	0	–	1	1	0	3	4
D	2	0	1	–	2	0	5	3
E	1	0	1	0	–	0	2	5=
F	2	2	2	2	2	–	10	1

Figure 2.1 A paired comparison

The advantage of paired comparison ranking over normal ranking is that it is easier to compare one job with another rather than having to make multi-comparisons. But it cannot overcome the fundamental objections to any form of whole-job ranking – that no defined standards for judging relative worth are provided and it is not an acceptable method of assessing equal value. There is also a limit to the number of jobs that can be compared using this method – to evaluate 50 jobs requires 1,225 comparisons.

Paired comparisons can also be used analytically to compare jobs on a factor by factor basis.

Job classification

Job classification is the process of slotting jobs into grades by comparing the whole job with a scale in the form of a hierarchy of grade definitions. It is based on an initial definition of the number and characteristics of the grades into which jobs will be placed. The grade definitions may refer to such job characteristics as skill, decision making and responsibility. Job descriptions may be used which include information on the presence of those characteristics but the characteristics are not assessed separately when comparing the description with the grade definition.

Job classification is the most used form of non-analytical job evaluation because it is simple, easily understood and at least, in contrast to whole-job ranking, it provides some standards for making judgements in the form of the grade definitions. But:

- it cannot cope with complex jobs which will not fit neatly into one grade;

- the grade definitions tend to be so generalized that they may not be much help in evaluating borderline cases;

- it fails to deal with the problem of evaluating and grading jobs in dissimilar occupational or job families where the demands made on jobholders are widely different;

- grade definitions tend to be inflexible and unresponsive to changes affecting roles and job content;

▌ the grading system can perpetuate inappropriate hierarchies;

▌ because it is not an analytical system, it is not effective as a means of establishing comparable worth and does not provide a defence in equal value cases.

Job matching

Job matching, sometimes known as internal benchmarking, is what people often do intuitively when they are deciding on the value of jobs, although it has never been dignified in the job evaluation texts as a formal method of job evaluation. It simply means comparing the job under review with any internal job which is believed to be properly graded and paid and placing the job under consideration into the same grade as that job. The comparison is often made on a whole-job basis without analysing the jobs factor by factor. Job matching is often based on comparisons with 'generic role profiles', ie profiles that cover groups of roles that are essentially similar.

Job matching is likely to be more accurate and acceptable if it is founded on the comparison of roles against a defined set of factors, ie analytical factor comparison. This may mean matching a role profile prepared under the factor headings with a generic role profile using the same headings.

Job matching is perhaps the most common method of informal or semi-formal job evaluation. It can be used after an initial analytical job evaluation exercise as a means of allocating jobs into an established grade structure without going to the trouble of carrying out a separate analytical evaluation. It is frequently adopted as the normal method of grading jobs on a continuing basis. In these circumstances, the analytical job evaluation scheme has a supporting role but will be used to deal with special cases, for example new or significantly changed jobs, and to review job matching decisions to ensure that they are valid and do not create equal value problems.

The advantages of job matching are that:

▌ it can produce reasonable results as long as it is based on the comparison of accurate job descriptions or role profiles which have been prepared using the same analytical framework of factors;

▌ it can be used to implement a full job evaluation exercise where there are a large number of people in generic roles and these roles can safely be matched with an original analytical evaluation of a comparator role;

▌ it is simple and quick.

The disadvantages of job matching are that:

▌ it can rely on judgements which may be entirely subjective and could be hard to justify objectively;

▌ it depends on the identification of suitable benchmarks which are properly graded;

▌ the assumption that the comparisons are being made for generic roles may be incorrect – significant differences between roles may be glossed over and this could create inequities;

▌ there is a danger that the comparisons will simply perpetuate existing inequities;

▌ staff whose jobs have been 'matched' may feel that they have been short-changed;

▌ it would not be acceptable in equal value cases unless it can be proved that an analytical basis is used for the comparisons.

The advantages of job matching are compelling but these are formidable disadvantages. As a supplementary method of evaluation it is probably well established but it has to be explained and used with great care.

Market pricing

Market pricing is the process of assessing rates of pay by reference to the market rates for comparable jobs – external benchmarking. In conjunction with a formal job evaluation scheme, establishing market rates is a necessary part of a programme for developing a pay structure. However, the term market pricing in its extreme form is used to denote a process of directly pricing jobs on the basis of external relativities with no regard to internal relativities.

Market pricing can be done formally by the analysis of published pay surveys, participating in 'pay clubs', conducting special surveys, obtaining the advice of recruitment consultants and agencies and, more doubtfully, by studying advertisements. In its crudest form, market pricing simply means fixing the rate for a job at the level necessary to recruit or retain someone.

Objections to market pricing

Market pricing is a manifestation of the dubious saying that 'a job is worth what the market says it is worth'. This is dubious for three reasons. First, because it ignores the importance of internal equity; second, because it takes no account of the fact that the internal value of jobs and roles can be quite unrelated to their value in other organizations; and third, because it can perpetuate marketplace inequities.

The major objection to market pricing is that it can perpetuate discrimination against women or members of certain racial groups. If market rates for jobs generally held by women or people of one or more racial groups are depressed because of long-standing bias, then this will be reflected in the pay structure. A market pricing approach to valuing jobs is not analytical and as such may be discriminatory.

Market pricing is also flawed because it is based on the assumption that it is easy to get hold of comprehensive and accurate information on market rates. This assumption is ill-founded. For some jobs there may be no reliable market data. In such cases they have to be slotted into the pay structure and a more conventional evaluation scheme may be required to establish relativities between the jobs that can be market priced and those that cannot.

Market pricing can produce tensions between the principle of internal equity and comparable worth and the perceived need to be competitive. Even when job evaluation is used to determine grades and therefore pay ranges, market supplements may be paid or 'market groups' set up to enable the organization to attract and retain staff whose jobs are valued more highly in the marketplace. This is a potential source of inequity if the people who are paid higher market-governed rates tend to be men rather than women. That is why equal pay case law has ruled that such differentials should be 'objectively justified'.

Use of market pricing

Market pricing is used by firms that do not believe in job evaluation and think that the only basis for fixing rates of pay is what the market dictates. It is often adopted implicitly by companies that, for whatever reason, do not have a formal graded pay structure and use spot rates, that is, individual rates for jobs. These may be the rates at which employees have been recruited and are therefore the rates for the person rather than the job. The rates may be increased to reflect the market worth for an individual and therefore to help with retention. But they are still spot rates based on market comparabilities. Slightly more sophisticated firms may have a system of individual job ranges where there is a defined range of pay for a job but this range is built round a market-determined reference point.

Market pricing is often a common feature of broad-banding – the development of grade and pay structures which may have only five or six broad bands and where the range of pay is much greater than in the conventional structure which may have 10 to 12 relatively narrow grades. A typical broad-banded structure could have pay ranges where the maximum is 100 per cent above the minimum, while the width in a narrow-graded structure could be no more than 20 to 30 per cent. Broad-banded structures may indicate the rates for jobs as 'reference points' within the bands and sometimes rely entirely, or at least to a very large extent, on market pricing to locate those points. Issues concerning the use of job evaluation in conjunction with market pricing and the implications for equal pay in such structures are discussed in Chapter 9.

Job family structures as described in Chapter 9 are also sometimes designed to take account of market rates. A job family consists of jobs related by the activities carried out and the knowledge and skills required (eg marketing, IT) and a job family structure will have a separate grade structure for each family. These may be treated as 'market groups' in which different pay structures are adopted for job families such as IT to reflect market pressures. Again, this raises equal pay issues.

DESIGN AND PROCESS CRITERIA

It is necessary to distinguish between the design of a scheme and the process of operating it. Equal pay considerations have to be taken into account in both design and process.

Design principles

For an analytical scheme, the design principles are that:

- the scheme should be based on a thorough analysis to determine what factors are appropriate;

- the scheme should facilitate impartial judgements of relative job size;

- the factors used in the scheme should cover the whole range of jobs to be evaluated at all levels without favouring any particular type of job or occupation and without discriminating on the grounds of gender, race, disability or for any other reason – the scheme should fairly measure features of female-dominated jobs as well as male-dominated jobs;

- through the use of common factors and methods of analysis and evaluation, the scheme should enable benchmarking to take place of the relativities between jobs in different functions or job families;

- the factors should be clearly defined and differentiated – there should be no double counting;

- the levels should be defined and graduated carefully;

- gender bias must be avoided in the choice of factors, the wording of factor and level definitions and the factor weightings – statistical checks should be carried out to identify any bias.

Process principles

The process principles are that:

- the scheme should be transparent; everyone concerned should know how it works – the basis upon which the evaluations are produced;

- appropriate proportions of women, those from ethnic minorities and people with disabilities should be involved in the process of job evaluation;

- the quality of role analysis should be monitored to ensure that analyses produce accurate and relevant information which will inform the job evaluation process and will not be biased;

- consistency checks should be built into operating procedures;

- the outcomes of evaluations should be examined to ensure that gender or any other form of bias has not occurred;

- particular care is necessary to ensure that the outcomes of job evaluation do not simply replicate the existing hierarchy – it is to be expected that a job evaluation exercise will challenge present relativities;

- all those involved in role analysis and job evaluation should be thoroughly trained in the operation of the scheme and in how to avoid bias;

- special care should be taken in developing a grade structure following a job evaluation exercise to ensure that grade boundaries are placed appropriately and that the allocation of jobs to grades is not in itself discriminatory;

- there should be scope for the review of evaluations and for appeals against gradings;

▌ the scheme should be reviewed regularly to ensure that it is being operated properly and that it is still fit for its purpose.

CRITERIA FOR CHOICE

The main criteria for selecting a scheme which emerge from these principles are that it should be:

▌ *analytical* – it should be based on the analysis and evaluation of the degree to which various defined elements or factors are present in a job;

▌ *thorough in analysis and capable of impartial application* – the scheme should have been carefully constructed to ensure that its analytical framework is sound and appropriate in terms of all the jobs it has to cater for, and it should also have been tested and trialled to check that it can be applied impartially to those jobs;

▌ *appropriate* – it should cater for the particular demands made on all the jobs to be covered by the scheme;

▌ *comprehensive* – the scheme should be applicable to all the jobs in the organization covering all categories of staff, and the factors should be common to all those jobs; there should therefore be a single scheme which can be used to assess relativities across different occupations or job families and to enable benchmarking to take place as required;

▌ *transparent* – the processes used in the scheme, from the initial role analysis through to the grading decision, should be clear to all concerned, and if computers are used, information should not be perceived as being processed in a 'black box';

▌ *non-discriminatory* – the scheme must meet equal pay for work of equal value requirements.

3

Job evaluation now

A survey conducted by E-Reward in late 2002[1] produced up-to-date and revealing information on what is happening to job evaluation in the UK from 236 respondents (83 per cent from private sector organizations and 17 per cent from employers in the public services and voluntary sectors). The main findings of the research are summarized below.

INTEREST IN JOB EVALUATION

Interest in job evaluation persists in spite of the negative views of many commentators. Although less than half (44 per cent) of the respondents to the survey used formal job evaluation, 45 per cent of those without a scheme intended to introduce one. Only 5 per cent had abandoned job evaluation. Formal job evaluation is much more common in the public and voluntary sectors (68 per cent of respondents) than in the private sector (39 per cent of respondents).

JOB EVALUATION SCHEMES

Analytical schemes were used by 89 per cent of the respondents. Of those, 70 per cent use points-factor rating. The most popular non-analytical approach was job classification. Thirty-seven per cent of the schemes are home grown while 37 per cent use a proprietary brand and 26 per cent use a hybrid or tailored version of a proprietary brand. Eighty-three per cent of the proprietary brand schemes are the Hay Guide Chart-profile method. Organizations opting for a proprietary brand did so because of its credibility and, especially with Hay, its link to a market rate data base. Organizations opting for a home-grown approach did so because they believe this would ensure that it could be shaped to meet the strategic needs of the organization and fit its technology, structure, work processes and business objectives. A minority of respondents mentioned the scope for aligning the scheme with their competency framework.

Only 28 per cent of respondents with job evaluation schemes used computers to aid evaluation. The main application was the calculation of job scores, mentioned by nine in ten of those with computerized systems (89 per cent), followed by processing the answers to job analysis questionnaires (55 per cent). Half the respondents used software to sort and analyse job evaluation scores across employee or job groups. By far the majority of those with job evaluation (74 per cent) have only one scheme. The interest in conducting equal pay reviews was encouraging – plans to conduct a review were being made by 72 per cent of responding organizations with 500 or more employees and 56 per cent of those with less than 500 employees.

FACTOR PLANS

An analysis of the factor lists provided by respondents in 39 schemes showed that the total number of factors listed by the organizations was 271, although many are similar. The range of factors in the schemes was from three to fourteen and the average number of factors was seven. The most frequently used factors were:

1. knowledge and skills;

2. communications and contacts;

3. decision making;

4. impact;

5. people management;

6. freedom to act;

7. working environment;

8. responsibility for financial resources.

REASONS FOR USING JOB EVALUATION

Respondents believed strongly that the main reasons for using a formal approach to job evaluation were: 1) to provide a basis for the design and maintenance of a rational and equitable pay structure; 2) to help manage job relativities; 3) to assimilate newly created jobs into the structure; 4) to ensure equitable pay structure, and 5) to ensure the principle of equal pay for work of equal value.

VIEWS ABOUT JOB EVALUATION

Respondents had mixed views about their schemes. Seventeen per cent were highly satisfied, 53 per cent were reasonably well satisfied, 19 per cent were not very satisfied and 6 per cent were totally dissatisfied. (There was no answer from the remaining respondents.)

The highly satisfied respondents' comments included: 'Provides us with a fair and equitable structure into which we can fit our reward strategy', 'It's objective, transparent and consistent', 'Open scheme with employee involvement provides felt-fair outcomes in terms of internal ranking/differentials and link to external market for reward comparison'. The comments of those who were totally dissatisfied included: 'It has outlived its usefulness and is no longer fair', 'The scheme has decayed to the point of total manipulation on the part of managers and trade union representatives', 'System has been operating far too long and discrepancies appeared. There's a push towards higher grading... and it's not adapted to the way we manage the business now'.

TIPS FROM PRACTITIONERS ON THE DESIGN, INTRODUCTION AND MAINTENANCE OF JOB EVALUATION SCHEMES

The practitioners who responded to the survey produced a number of practical tips on the development and use of job evaluation, as set out in the three boxes below.

Box 3.1   Tips on scheme design
- 'Simplify.'
- 'Make schemes less wordy and subjective.'
- 'Make sure scheme covers whole organization.'
- 'Consider factor definitions more carefully.'
- 'Use a computer-based system.'
- 'Allow for flexibility and creating new job families.'
- 'Use more meaningful and less generic job descriptions.'
- 'Define clearer boundaries between bands.'
- 'Move towards job families and wider bands.'
- 'Clarify promotion routes and career paths.'

Box 3.2 Tips on scheme introduction

- 'Prepare the technical work within HR. Present to senior managers with a good description of the advantages to them (some real-life examples they can relate to). Then communicate the project to the whole organization (a specific project team needs to be working on the plan). Use different media to give information to employees.'
- 'Overkill communication.'
- 'Explain more thoroughly.'
- 'Involve all stakeholders early on.'
- 'Try to ensure a greater understanding of the scheme at an earlier stage.'
- 'Gain greater business buy-in and support so that it is seen as a business tool rather than an HR process.'
- 'Widen pool of trained evaluators.'
- 'Set more reasonable timescales to manage employee expectations.'
- 'It should be run like a project with specific success criteria and regular reviews; no one should be afraid to amend it as appropriate rather than letting the job evaluation system run the organization.'
- 'Introduce through a rigorous process of pilot testing.'

Box 3.3 Tips on scheme maintenance

- 'Need to ensure that regular reviews of scheme are built in.'
- 'Provide adequate training for those operating the scheme.'
- 'Ensure trained evaluators don't get rusty.'
- 'Use IT in a smarter way.'
- 'Again, ensure better communications with employees.'
- 'More line accountability and involvement.'
- 'Find a less time-consuming way of managing it.'
- 'Have a more robust process for challenging and slotting new roles.'
- 'Maintain better systems for record keeping and adopt smoother processes.'
- 'Ensure tighter policing and provide clearer rationale.'

Reference

1. E-Reward.co.uk: Research Report no. 7, January 2003

4

Equal pay for work of equal value

BACKGROUND

The sub-title of this book is *A guide to achieving equal pay*. In recent years, job evaluation has become regarded as a vehicle for moving towards equal pay between men and women, but this was not always so. This chapter describes the transition and explains in broad terms how job evaluation schemes can be designed and implemented in accordance with principles of equity and equal value. More detailed explanation is provided in subsequent chapters.

Job evaluation schemes were not originally designed to achieve equal pay for work of equal value. Indeed, when job evaluation techniques were first developed in the United States in the 1930s and 1940s, there was little interest in and no national legislation on equality issues. Job evaluation systems were constructed to:

▌ provide an alternative quantitative measure for the work of clerical, administrative and managerial employees to the

work study measurement systems then increasingly
common for production workers;

▨ reflect market rates for clerical, administrative and
managerial jobs;

▨ rationalize pre-existing organizational hierarchies.

The schemes of that time reflected these aims. They measured and
emphasized job features, such as qualifications and quantifiable
skills, scope for initiative (position in hierarchy), decision making
and problem solving, numbers of staff managed and size of budget
controlled.

They also reflected historical collective bargaining arrangements,
with schemes generally being developed for a single bargaining
group. This could result in there being several schemes in operation
within a large organization – for example, for administrative and
clerical staff; for managers; possibly also for technical employees;
and later for production workers also.

Such schemes were introduced into the UK in the late 1940s, initially into insurance and other finance sector companies and over
the succeeding decades across parts of the private sector and, from
the early 1970s onwards, into the public sector. These schemes are
still operative in many organizations.

Early job evaluation schemes were implemented in the UK into
organizations that often had separate and lower rates of pay for
women. Before 1970, it was common practice for there to be lower
rates of pay for women, even where women and men did the same
or comparable jobs. In the 1960s, for example, at the Ford Motor
Company, as in many other private sector manufacturing companies, there were four rates covering production workers:

1. skilled male rate;

2. semi-skilled male rate;

3. unskilled male rate;

4. women's rate.

The women's rate applied to production sewing machinists, who were paid less than male workers who swept the factory floor or supplied parts to the production line. In large part as a result of a strike by the Ford machinists over their pay and grading under a new pay structure resulting from a job evaluation exercise, the Equal Pay Act was passed in 1970. It did not come into force until 1975, giving employers five years to eliminate lower rates of pay for women.

EQUAL PAY LEGISLATION IN THE UK

The 1970 Equal Pay Act effectively outlawed separate rates of pay for women by introducing an implied equality clause into all contracts of employment. It also provided two grounds on which an applicant could take a claim to an Industrial (now Employment) Tribunal for equal pay with a comparator of opposite gender: 1) 'like work', meaning the same or very similar work; 2) 'work rated as equivalent' under a job evaluation 'study'.

The 'work rated as equivalent' clause was actually brought in to prevent a repetition of the experience of the Ford sewing machinists, who received only 85 per cent of the evaluated grade rate for the job. However, as this situation is unlikely to recur, it has been used in other contexts, for example when a job evaluation exercise has been carried out but the results not implemented. These have required Tribunals to consider what constituted a 'valid' job evaluation scheme for the purposes of the legislation – essentially that it should be complete and jointly agreed between management and unions.[1]

The UK was unaffected by European pay equity legislation until it joined the European Community in 1972. Article 119 of the EC founding Treaty of Rome of 1957 (now subsumed and expanded as Article 142 of the Treaty of Maastricht) said that men and women should receive equal pay for equal work – in order to achieve what is often described as a 'level playing field' in terms of wages. Article 119 was extended by the Equal Pay Directive of 1975, which stated that:

▮ men and women should receive equal pay for work of equal value;

▮ job classification systems (which is Euro-English for any formal grading system and thus encompasses job evaluation schemes) should be fair and non-discriminatory;

▮ EC member states should take steps to implement the equal pay principle.

The European Commission prosecuted the UK government before the European Court of Justice (ECJ) for not having legislation to implement the concept of equal pay for work of equal value. The ECJ found against the UK on the grounds that the 'work rated as equivalent' clause applied only where there was a job evaluation scheme and did not cover all those outside schemes.[2] As a result, Mrs Thatcher's Conservative government was required to implement the Equal Pay (Equal Value) Amendment Regulations, which introduced a third ground for an applicant to apply to a Tribunal for equal pay: 3) 'work of equal value', when a comparison is made under headings 'such as effort, skill and decision'.

Those drafting the amending legislation clearly intended that the Independent Expert, who is appointed by the Tribunal (from a panel administered by ACAS) to make the comparative assessment, should use job evaluation techniques to carry out what is effectively a mini-job-evaluation exercise on applicant and comparator jobs.

The amended legislation stipulates that where both applicant and comparator jobs have already been evaluated under a fair and non-discriminatory job evaluation scheme, the Tribunal should not further consider the case, unless the applicant can show that the evaluation of either job is fundamentally flawed.

THE IMPACT OF THE LEGISLATION ON JOB EVALUATION PRACTICE IN THE UK

The 'equal value' provision and accompanying 'job evaluation study' defence to equal value claims are currently under review, but have impacted on job evaluation in the UK in a number of ways:

▮ The 'job evaluation study' defence, together with the fact that very few schemes have been determined by Tribunals to be discriminatory, has encouraged the spread of job evaluation, particularly into female-dominated organizations and sectors. This is one of the reasons why job evaluation has become more prevalent, in spite of criticisms of it and predictions of its demise (see Chapter 1, 'The case for and against job evaluation').

▌ The 'job evaluation study' defence applies only where applicant and comparator jobs are covered by the same job evaluation scheme. As a result, new job evaluation schemes are more likely to apply across all or most jobs in an organization, perhaps excluding only senior managers, rather than to a single collective bargaining group.

▌ This has changed the nature of job evaluation schemes, from having a limited number of specific factors, directed at particular types of work, to schemes with a larger number of more generic factors, applicable to a wider range of jobs.

▌ The legal references in UK and European legislation to job evaluation and all of the above developments have led to the job evaluation version of navel gazing – with a view to identifying features which make a scheme more, or less, discriminatory. In the absence of any comprehensive legal precedents on job evaluation schemes, both the European Union and the domestic Equal Opportunities Commission have produced codes of practice on equal pay, including job evaluation.[3] The latter has also produced specific guidance on job evaluation, in checklist form, the most recent version of which is on the EOC Web site at: www.eoc.org.uk.

IMPACT OF EQUAL PAY LEGISLATION ON JOB EVALUATION DESIGN

The main thrust of both the EU codes of practice and the EOC checklist is to ensure that any job evaluation scheme is suitable for the jobs it is intended to cover and is designed to measure fairly all significant features of jobs typically carried out by women as well as of those generally carried out by men. The scheme must be analytical: this was confirmed by the Court of Appeal in its decision in the case of *Bromley v H&J Quick Ltd* [[1988] IRLR 249 CA] (see also below).

In broad terms the potential sins in this area are:

▪ *Omission* – of job features more commonly found in jobs carried out by women, for example manual dexterity, interpersonal skills, 'caring' responsibilities, organizing skills.

In the case of *Rummler v Dato-Druck GmbH* [[1987] IRLR 32 ECJ], the ECJ made clear that this did not mean that factors likely to favour one gender over the other had to be omitted. But, if a scheme included a factor likely to advantage the jobs of men, for example physical effort, then there should also be factors to measure comparable features of typically women's jobs, for instance stamina or manual dexterity. In the case in question, the applicant had complained that her employer's job evaluation scheme was discriminatory because it included a factor to measure physical effort, against which her job scored relatively lowly. The ECJ said this was acceptable as long as it is designed also to 'take into account other criteria for which female employees may show particular aptitude'.

▪ *Double counting* – of job features under more than one factor heading. For example, in a critique in 1987 of the GLWC job evaluation scheme developed in the early 1970s to apply to clerical, administrative, professional and technical jobs in local government, Lorraine Paddison found that some features – professional status; managerial role; position in the status hierarchy – were measured under a number of headings.[4] She noted, for example, in relation to managerial responsibility, that: 'Apart from the Supervisory Responsibility factor, a managerial responsibility in addition to a professional role is explicitly rewarded at high levels in Education, Decisions, Supervision Received and Work Complexity.'

▌ *Elision* (sometimes called Compression) – of more than one job feature under a single factor heading, with the result that one of the features dominates in terms of the assessment process.

For example, trying to measure all forms of responsibility under a single factor heading can result in some forms, often people-related responsibilities, being disadvantaged by comparison with finance or other physical-resource-related responsibilities.

These sins can be avoided by identifying factors which, between them, measure all significant job features and are of broadly comparable scope (see Chapter 7, Identifying and defining factors). An illustration of this is found in the local government NJC Job Evaluation Scheme, which was designed to support grading reviews under the Single Status Agreement of 1997 and to cover previous manual worker jobs as well as the APT&C group mentioned above. The main features of this scheme are set out in tabular form in Appendix 1.

A revealing comparison between the factors of the GLWC scheme criticized by Lorraine Paddison and those of the NJC job evaluation scheme is shown in Table 4.1.

Table 4.1 Factor choice: local government job evaluation schemes of the past and the future

More discriminatory local government (GWLC) job evaluation scheme (1971)	Less discriminatory local government (NJC) job evaluation scheme (1997)
1. Education	1. Knowledge
2. Experience	2. Mental skills
9. Creative work	3. Interpersonal/Communication skills
8. Contacts	4. Physical skills
5. Supervision received	5. Initiative and independence
6. Work complexity	6. Physical effort
3. Supervisory responsibility	7. Mental effort
4. Decisions	8. Emotional effort
7. Assets	9. Responsibility for people
	10. Responsibility for supervising other employees
	11. Responsibility for financial resources
	12. Responsibility for physical resources
	13. Working conditions

Although the absence from the older GLWC job evaluation scheme of factors measuring physical effort and working conditions might be excused by the omission from its scope of manual jobs, the exclusion of factors to measure responsibilities for local authority clients and members of the public, physical skills and emotional demands cannot be so easily justified.

Other potential sources of discrimination highlighted in the Codes are also illustrated by the comparison of the two local government schemes:

- *Measurement of knowledge requirements*: the GLWC scheme uses two quantifiable factors – Education and Experience, which concentrate respectively on formal qualifications and years of experience in post. Both of these are likely to favour male employees over female employees undertaking comparable work (who in the past have been less likely to be formally qualified and have had different work and career patterns from men). The NJC job evaluation scheme adopts instead a single factor, which measures the nature of the actual knowledge required to undertake the work (using qualifications only as an indicator of this demand).

- *Scoring and weighting*: while the level scores for some factors in the GLWC scheme increase by equal steps, others do not. For example, in the education factor the level scores are: 10; 20; 30; 45; 55; 85; 105. The points steps are thus 10; 10; 15; 10; 30; 20. There is no obvious justification or logic to this pattern and it lays the scheme open to the challenge that it was designed to achieve specific, possibly discriminatory, outcomes.

As the table in Appendix 1 shows, the NJC job evaluation scheme, in contrast, has scores increasing by equal steps throughout. This has an obvious logic and is justified on the basis that the level definitions were designed to represent equal steps in demand. Other scoring systems may be justifiable, if they are also logical and the justification is transparent.

Knowledge is the most heavily weighted area in both schemes, but in the NJC scheme weighting is based on a set of principles (see table in Appendix 1), while there is no obvious rationale for the GLWC scheme weighting, other than to replicate a previous organizational hierarchy. Issues of scoring and weighting in the design of a job evaluation scheme are further considered in Chapter 7.

IMPACT OF EQUAL PAY LEGISLATION ON IMPLEMENTATION OF JOB EVALUATION

The focus of the EU and EOC guidance in respect of implementing job evaluation is to ensure that all significant features of jobs carried out by women as well as those undertaken by men are first 'captured' as part of the process, and then fairly evaluated. The methods recommended for achieving this are:

- *Use of a detailed job questionnaire:* job evaluation on the basis of a traditional organizational job description is likely to be unsatisfactory, because it leaves evaluators to use their own experience or make assumptions when assessing jobs against factors for which no information is provided.

   The preferred approach is to collect job information from jobholders and their supervisors or line managers by means of a structured questionnaire, which asks specific questions, requiring factual answers, under each of the job evaluation factor headings. This pre-analysis of job information, although time consuming to do properly, also makes for more efficient evaluation by reducing the time evaluators spend identifying the information they need and debating what is relevant. Fully computerized schemes (see Chapter 8) also adopt this approach by asking specific questions under each factor heading.

- *Training in avoidance of bias* for job analysts/facilitators and evaluators. This both assists in avoiding discrimination in the implementation of job evaluation and demonstrates to others that efforts have been made to avoid bias (see Chapter 6).

▨ *Avoidance of traditional 'slotting' techniques:* in even a medium-sized organization, it is time consuming to evaluate the job of every individual employee separately. In a large organization, it is impossible. Historically, therefore, it was common practice in larger organizations to evaluate only a benchmark sample of jobs and to 'slot' other jobs against the benchmark through some form of whole-job comparison. However, in its decision in the case of *Bromley & Others v H.&J. Quick,* the Court of Appeal said that the applicant and comparator jobs which had been 'slotted' in this way had not been analysed and evaluated under the scheme in question, so were not covered by the 'job evaluation study' defence. There was not such a study 'where the jobs of the women and their comparators were slotted into the structure on a 'whole job' basis and no comparison was made by reference to the selected factors between the demands made on the individual workers under the selected headings'.

This decision has significant implications for job evaluation in large organizations, as it implies that all employees should be attached to a job description, which has either been analysed and evaluated, or, at minimum, has been matched to an evaluated benchmark job, using an analytical process.

▨ *Monitoring of outcomes*: the initial job evaluation exercise and subsequent appeals should be monitored for their impact on male- and female-dominated jobs. Other things being equal, one would expect a new job evaluation scheme to result in some upward movement of female-dominated jobs, particularly those that show typical features of work carried out by women, relative to other jobs, as historical pay discrimination is eliminated.

References

1. *Eaton Ltd v Nuttall* [1977] IRLR 71 EAT: a valid job evaluation study must satisfy 'the test of being thorough in analysis and capable of impartial application'.

Arnold v Beecham Group Ltd [1982] IRLR 307 EAT: 'there is no complete job evaluation study unless and until the parties who have agreed to carry out the study have accepted its validity. However, it is not the stage of implementing the study by using it as the basis of the payment of remuneration that makes it complete; it is the stage at which it is accepted as a study.'

O'Brien v Sim-Chem Ltd [1980] IRLR 373 HL: Once a job evaluation study has been undertaken and has resulted in a conclusion that the job of a woman is of equal value with that of a man, then a comparison of their respective terms and conditions is made feasible and... The equality clause can take effect. It is not necessary for the pay structure to have been adjusted as a result of the conclusions of the job evaluation study.'

2. Commission of the European Communities v United Kingdom of Great Britain and Northern Ireland [1982] IRLR 333 ECJ

3. European Commission, Employment & Social Affairs: *A code of practice on the implementation of equal pay for work of equal value for men and women:* Luxembourg, 1996

   Equal Opportunities Commission: *Code of Practice on Equal Pay:* Manchester, 1997 (currently being revised)

4. Paddison, Lorraine: *Job evaluation and equal value – a study of white collar job evaluation in London local authorities:* London Equal Value Steering Group (LEVEL), September 1987

5

Equal pay reviews

As described in Chapter 4, UK organizations have a legal obligation to provide equal pay for equal work that is free from sex bias. In order to know whether this legal obligation is being met, organizations need to understand whether their practices and policies are achieving this outcome. The Equal Opportunity Commission's (EOC's) *Code of Practice on Equal Pay*[1] says that an internal review is 'the most appropriate method of ensuring that a pay system delivers equal pay free from sex bias'.

This chapter describes the equal pay review process (sometimes termed equal pay audits). However, it does not intend to replicate the comprehensive guidance that is available through other sources such as the EOC *Equal Pay Review Kit*[2] or the CIPD *Equal Pay Guide*[3]. It focuses instead on how organizations can respond to the analysis challenges presented by equal pay reviews in the context of their existing approach(es) to valuing jobs.

As highlighted in Chapter 4, equal pay legislation deals with the analysis and diagnosis of equal pay issues between women and men. Equal pay legislation requires equal pay to be given for 'equal work'. Equal work is:

▌ like work – work which is the same or broadly similar;

▌ work rated as equivalent – work which has been evaluated similarly using an analytical job evaluation scheme;

▌ work of equal value – work which is of broadly equal value when compared under headings such as effort, skill and decisions.

Pay differences are allowable only if the reason for them is not related to the sex of the jobholder. The same principles of fairness and equity should, of course, apply to other potentially discriminating characteristics such as racial group and disability. However, for the sake of simplicity this chapter refers mainly to gender.

WHY CONDUCT EQUAL PAY REVIEWS?

Before looking at the equal pay review process, this section considers how equal pay reviews are instrumental in moving the equity agenda forwards, and the benefits that organizations can expect from conducting them.

Despite UK equal pay legislation of over 30 years' standing, an EOC equal pay taskforce, reporting in 2001, found that there was still an 18 per cent difference between hourly pay rates of full-time male and female employees. The difference was even more pronounced for part-time employees. There are a number of reasons for this, including different career paths for men and women. However, the taskforce estimated that up to half the difference was due to pay discrimination.

Whether or not this figure is accurate, the taskforce also found that there was a distinct lack of evidence to support employers' commonly held view that there was no gender gap in their own organization. This lack of evidence was actually due to the fact that very few organizations had taken steps to investigate the issue, with many of them being unaware of the *Code of Practice on Equal Pay* and its encouragement to conduct reviews, first published in 1997 (subsequently updated in 2003).

The taskforce therefore recommended that organizations should be legally obliged to carry out regular equal pay reviews. As a result of the Kingsmill review,[4] set up subsequently to look at non-statutory ways to encourage equality, the government came down in favour of a voluntary approach, while requiring government departments and agencies to conduct reviews by April 2003. The EOC also let it be known that they would monitor whether voluntary reviews were indeed taking place – making it clear that they would lobby hard for compulsory reviews if organizations were slow to respond on a voluntary basis. Trade unions have also been instrumental in keeping the issue at the forefront of the pay agenda.

Purpose

The purpose of equal pay reviews is to:

▌ establish whether any gender-related pay inequities have arisen;

▌ analyse the nature of any inequities and diagnose the cause(s);

▌ determine what action is required to deal with any inequities that are revealed.

In doing so they should give organizations confidence about whether they are meeting their legal obligations with respect to equal pay for equal work. There is also the broader benefit from being seen to apply a fair and equitable reward system, and the positive impact this has on employee perceptions and satisfaction.

With effect from 2003, equal pay reviews will also support organizations' ability to respond to employee requests for information about their pay practices in accordance with the 2002 Employment Act. This provides for a statutory equal pay questionnaire to help individuals who believe that they may not have received equal pay to obtain information from their employer on whether this is the case, and why, before deciding whether to submit an equal pay claim.

Despite the resurgence of publicity about equal pay since the late 1990s, the E-Reward research published in early 2003 revealed that many organizations remained unfamiliar with the purpose and benefits of equal pay reviews. There was also a lack of understanding about the possible sources of pay inequality.

However, some organizations openly admitted that their reward practices may not be robust owing to internal management processes:

> 'The company is privately owned and what the board says goes.'

Other respondents described a range of practices to explain where they considered their defence to equal pay claims rested: for example, the following two comments describe a market-based approach:

> 'The organizational structure at present is pretty simple... There is therefore limited exposure to "equal value" as the roles are benchmarked against their own industry norms.'

> '[we] will use salary survey methodology as a proxy. My understanding is this has already been used successfully to defend an equal pay claim.'

Even though market differentials are commonly cited as a potential justification for pay differentials, there is no such thing as an automatic market defence to an equal pay claim. As with all equal pay claims, any market-based defence will be looked at on its merits. Table 5.1 gives an indication of the kind of tests that might be applied to such a market-based defence.

Other comments describe how organizations seek to achieve fairness through having a robust approach to allocating jobs to a grade structure:

> 'Grades are evaluated and "levelled" by a committee of the senior management team.'

However, no matter how sound the process is for allocating jobs to grades, one of the biggest challenges to organizations is to pay fairly within grades. As described in Chapter 4, many organizations have responded to the equal pay challenge by maintaining or introducing analytical job evaluation schemes, on the assumption that if jobs are evaluated into grades using an analytical process, there is a robust defence to an equal pay claim. In part this is true; however, one of the purposes of equal pay reviews is to push the boundaries of analysis and action further – by requiring organizations to address actual pay gaps, even where the gaps occur within a single grade.

PLANNING A REVIEW

Before embarking on the data collection and analysis that are essential parts of an equal pay review, it is necessary to decide on the scope of the review: whether it should focus on gender only, or include other possible areas of pay inequity such as racial groups and those with disabilities. It is certainly advisable to consider the conduct and outcomes of an equal pay review in the context of all the other equality policies, procedures and processes in the organization. The review should cover employees on different employment terms, specifically part-time and hourly paid staff, if there are any, and those on short-term contracts or contracts of unspecified duration as well as full-time staff.

Part of the planning process will inevitably involve consideration of how to source and access the data that will be needed to feed the analysis. The initial data required may well sit across payroll and the HR database. The data for follow-up analyses may rest in individual files, or reside in the memory of longer-serving staff – if it exists at all. Issues that have come up in equal pay reviews include data that is not retrievable without HR support, data not collected in standardized form and the need to convert data from multiple sources onto a common database in order to generate reports.

Some software tools are available to support analyses. These range from database tools that enable data to be imported from a range of sources to generate pay gap analyses, such as the E-Review *Equal Pay Review Toolkit*, to more sophisticated tools that allow for a broader range of analysis possibilities using different data cuts, including the tool developed by Link. What is clear is that analysis needs will vary from one organization to the next and it is not always possible to specify in advance what analyses will be needed. Therefore, advice to organizations planning to replace their HR database is that one criterion should be the flexibility of customized reporting to support future equal pay review analyses.

There are other process decisions to be made – for example, about how intensive the review should be and at what point staff or unions should be involved. These process decisions are all well covered in the EOC *Equal Pay Review Toolkit* and other sources.

THE EQUAL PAY REVIEW PROCESS

Although the EOC *Equal Pay Review Toolkit* describes a five-stage process, there are essentially three main stages to an equal pay review:

1. *Analysis*: this involves collecting and analysing relevant data to identify any gender (pay) gaps.

2. *Diagnosis*: the process of reviewing gender gaps, understanding why they have occurred and what remedial action might be required if the differences cannot be objectively justified.

3. *Action*: agreeing and enacting an action plan that eliminates any inequalities.

The remainder of this chapter describes briefly these main stages, and then looks in more detail at some analysis options, based around an organization's existing approach to valuing jobs.

Stage one: analysis

This stage involves collecting and analysing pay and benefits practices and policies in order to test the extent of any differences in policy or application that might lead to unequal pay between men and women. There are three elements to this analysis stage:

1. Review the organization's equal pay policy

This is the most straightforward part of the initial analysis. It involves establishing whether or not an equal pay policy exists. If there is one, the organization should:

- compare the policy with the model policy set out in the EOC *Code of Practice on Equal Pay* (the policy is reproduced in Appendix 2);

- examine the extent to which it has been communicated internally;

- identify who is responsible for implementing the policy and what steps have been taken to ensure that it has been implemented.

Where there is no existing equal pay policy, the EOC model can be used as a basis for establishing one.

2. Pay analysis

This is about generating the first set of statistics that will help to indicate whether or not an organization may have an equal pay issue, and the extent to which further analysis will be needed. The analysis requirements are discussed later in this chapter.

3. Benefits comparison

This involves establishing the extent to which men and women have access to, and on average receive, equal benefits for equal work, such as pensions, sick pay, medical insurance, company cars and holidays. Benefits design, eligibility criteria and actual practice will need to be examined.

Benefits comparison is an essential part of the analysis phase because, although the publicity surrounding equal pay reviews focuses mainly on cash reward, equal pay legislation allows comparison to be made in respect of any remuneration item. There is no 'total remuneration' concept in equal pay law. This means that an equal pay claim can be submitted in respect of any remuneration item, where an individual feels that they are not being fairly treated in comparison with a colleague of the opposite sex doing equal work – even if their total remuneration package is worth the same.

Stage two: diagnosis

The aim of stage two is to establish the nature of any inequities and their causes with the intent of establishing whether the difference in pay is genuinely due to a material difference between the man's and the woman's jobs rather than due to their gender. The review should first seek explanations of why the gap exists and then establish the extent to which the gap can be objectively justified. This stage involves delving into the data, using intuition and judgement about where to focus effort, in order not to be overwhelmed by the mass of options for further analysis.

If this diagnostic phase suggests that any pay differences are gender based, the remedial action needed to rectify the situation should feed into stage three. Appendix 3 gives examples of the types of analyses and issues that could arise from this diagnostic phase, together with the remedial actions that may be required.

Stage three: action

Any issues that have been identified in phase two must be remedied. The course of action that will remove pay gaps must be defined, planned and implemented. The action plan should incorporate proposals on:

- introducing or amending an equal pay policy if necessary;

- the steps required to remove pay gaps;

- how future bias can be eliminated by changing the processes, rules or practices that gave rise to unequal pay;

- a programme for implementing change;

- accountabilities for drawing up and implementing the plan;

- how employee representatives or recognized trade unions should be involved in preparing and implementing the plan;

- the arrangements for monitoring the implementation of the plan and for evaluating outcomes.

With respect to how long an organization should take to address any inequities, the answer depends on the scale of change that is needed; the causes and costs involved in rectifying inequities are wide and varied. However, the timetable should be realistic in the light of change required, while demonstrating an immediate intention to implement change. In the interim the organization remains at risk of an equal pay claim – the intent to redress the difference is not sufficient to avoid a claim.

It is, of course, important to address both the cause and the effect of the inequity. For example, if the cause of pay differences within grades rests in an organization's recruitment processes, the short-term remedy may be to rectify existing pay differentials – but to avoid the situation arising again, more fundamental issues will need to be addressed relating to the recruitment process, perhaps including actions such as manager training and generating new guidelines on how to set recruitment salaries.

ANALYSING PAY

The rest of this chapter focuses on the types of pay analyses that may be involved in an equal pay review. In particular, it focuses on the initial analyses that are needed to check whether there appears to be a gender-related pay gap. The nature of analyses that are possible will be affected by the existing pay and grading structure. Some preparatory analysis of the employee population is needed before the statistical analyses can start.

Categorizing employees

The employee population must be broken down into categories that are meaningful for analysis purposes. This means identifying the occupational groupings that are needed in order to generate initial statistical analyses of potential gender pay gaps, for example by 'like work' or grade. It also requires converting the pay data for all employees onto a common basis. In order to compare like with like, the contractual hours of all employees need to be converted to the same standard, eg hourly, weekly or annual pay. All elements of cash remuneration, including allowances and bonuses, need to be similarly converted.

Determining initial analysis options

In the experience of organizations that have undertaken equal pay reviews, this step can be the most difficult part of the process. This is determining what kind of analyses an organization is able to do in relation to the three definitions of equal work. These are:

▪ *Like work* – this means identifying jobs anywhere in the organization where the work is the same or broadly similar. Where there is no job evaluation, this is the only type of equal work comparison that can readily be made. Although this should be a straightforward comparison, there are potential pitfalls, such as over-reliance on unrepresentative job titles. If existing job titles are not a good guide, it might be necessary to recategorize jobs in order to arrive at who is doing 'like work'. One financial institution that created generic role titles while implementing broad banding found that their titles had become so broad that they did not support a 'like work' comparison. In order to conduct an equal pay review it therefore had to reanalyse roles to break them down into more meaningful groupings.

▪ *Work rated as equivalent* – this means work that has been rated as equivalent using the organization's own analytical job evaluation scheme. Clearly, analyses can only be readily applied where the organization has a job evaluation scheme that covers the whole organization.

▪ *Work of equal value* – this is the 'catch all' in equal pay legislation. It means that an equal pay claim can be brought by any employee where they believe that their job is of equal worth to any other role in the organization that is occupied by someone of the opposite sex. As with the 'work rated as equivalent' test, the only organizations that can readily conduct analyses under this heading are those with an organization-wide job evaluation scheme that enables different types of jobs to be compared using criteria that apply equally across the organization.

These last two definitions of equal pay rely on job evaluation, and to fully satisfy an equal pay test in law the scheme should be analytical (see Chapter 4). However, it is unrealistic to expect that every organization will introduce an analytical job evaluation in order to provide a legal defence to equal pay claims, even those organizations that aim to be fair and equitable employers. Decisions about how to value and reward jobs are based on a wide range of organizational and business factors, and organizations must balance the relative benefits and risks of alternative approaches, of which the ability to meet all the tests laid down in equal pay legislation are just one – albeit an important one.

However, it is reasonable to expect organizations to apply a range of tests in good faith that will enable them to be satisfied that their pay practices and outcomes are non-discriminatory. Some of these analysis options are discussed later in this chapter.

Undertaking the initial pay analyses

As a minimum, organizations need to be able to undertake straightforward statistical checks to investigate the percentage pay difference between men and women doing the same or similar ('like') work and thus define any 'pay gap' that exists.

To do this, women's base pay and total pay should be calculated as a percentage of men's pay for all incumbents doing like work. It is helpful to separate the calculation into the different elements of total earnings in order to see where any pay differences lie. As mentioned earlier, in order to compare like with like this analysis needs to be based on a standard norm, eg annual or hourly pay.

The aim is to establish the degree to which inequality exists in the form of a significant pay gap. The EOC recommends that a pay gap in favour of more than one gender of more than 5 per cent for one job is significant enough to warrant further investigation, as is a pattern of differences in favour of one group of 3 per cent or more (eg a pay gap in favour of men at all or most levels of the organization).

However, the guideline percentages are, at best, a rule of thumb. It is more important to get an understanding of the pattern of differences and to investigate suspected problem areas, even if the results do not lie within these guideline percentages. It is also important to remember that an individual can make a claim whatever the aggregate statistics say.

The discovery of a gender pay gap does not automatically mean that there is a problem. However, differences must be objectively justifiable – so further investigation will be needed to check whether this is so. If the reason for the pay difference is gender related, the law requires that the inequity is remedied.

If job evaluation is used on an organization-wide basis, it is possible to conduct pay gap analyses that meet all three equal work categories. This can be done by conducting both a like work and an organization-wide comparison between the pay for men and women in the same grade irrespective of their occupational groups. This is because where organizations use analytical job evaluation, different types of jobs on the same grade, defined in terms of a range of job evaluation scores, will generally be regarded as being of 'equal worth', thus enabling a pay gap analysis that covers all employees in the same grade.

However, this is unlikely to be a satisfactory assessment of equal worth where bands or grades are so broad that they include jobs with a wide range of responsibilities and skills. Where this is the case, it may be necessary to split the grades/bands into narrower groups. This can be done fairly easily using a points-factor scheme's total job scores, but will not be so straightforward where other job evaluation techniques have been used (eg classification), without some adaptation to the scheme or alternative approach to deriving additional levels. Of course, the type of job evaluation approach used also impacts on the perceived robustness of the equal worth comparison in the first place.

Where there is no organization-wide job evaluation scheme, further steps need to be taken by an organization if it wants to satisfy itself that there is no potential gender pay gap. The extent to which an organization may need to extend analysis beyond the initial 'like' work check will depend on a number of factors:

▪ the outcome of the 'like work' analysis;

▪ the extent to which it wants to explore the potential risk of an equal pay claim;

▪ the extent to which it wants to be seen as adhering to 'best practice' in conducting an equal pay review.

The options for extending the analysis depend both on the level of rigour that the organization wants to apply and the nature of existing remuneration arrangements. In particular, the options for further analysis will depend on whether:

- analytical job evaluation is used in one or more parts of the organization – and can be extended across the organization;

- analytical job evaluation is not normally used, but where the organization may be prepared to apply it purely for equal pay review purposes;

- the organization is not prepared to apply analytical job evaluation formally.

Options for analysis in each of these cases are described below.

Extend the existing job evaluation scheme

Where analytical job evaluation is used in at least one part of the organization, this should be reviewed to see whether it can be applied organization-wide. If the factors are reasonably broad and cover a span of job levels, it is likely to be possible to apply the scheme to jobs elsewhere in the organization. Alternatively, it may be possible to adapt the scheme to enable broader coverage, either by adding levels or making some changes to the factor definitions. All or a sample of jobs across the organization can then be evaluated as a desk exercise (even where the normal evaluation process includes employee and manager participation). The results from this exercise can then be used to conduct a pay gap analysis by categorizing jobs into levels based on total points scores. However, if the scheme is tailored to meet the needs of a specific specialist area such as research, this may be more difficult.

Where an existing scheme cannot be applied or adapted for organization-wide use, the alternative is to conduct some form of benchmarking across the organization using an alternative analytical scheme, as described below.

Apply analytical job evaluation for equal pay review purposes only

Even where an organization does not use an analytical scheme on an ongoing basis, analytical job evaluation techniques can be applied selectively, purely for the purpose of conducting an equal pay review and for monitoring for equal pay on an ongoing basis.

This can be done by:

▌ creating a simple in-house scheme; this approach involves little up-front monetary cost, but involves internal cost in terms of the development and analysis time;

▌ employing a consultancy that has a proprietary scheme to evaluate jobs on the organization's behalf;

▌ evaluating a sample of jobs over the Internet using a consultancy firm's proprietary scheme; this is a relatively new approach, but some reputable job evaluation providers, such as Link (see Chapter 8), offer this service at a significantly lower cost than engaging a consultancy firm to do the work in-house, although there is an internal time cost in terms of time needed to evaluate the jobs.

Assuming that an organization does not want to commit itself publicly to analytical job evaluation, these three exercises can all be undertaken as a background desk study, rather than through a more open evaluation process. The details of the approach taken may well depend on the availability of suitable job information for feeding into whichever approach is chosen. In order to keep the exercise within manageable boundaries, it may be sufficient to use a small team of managers or HR staff that have a broad knowledge of the organization to provide the relevant job information or to evaluate the jobs.

A number of organizations maintain an analytical job evaluation scheme in the background purely for internal monitoring, while using another job evaluation approach such as classification or role matching as the 'public' face of job evaluation. This supports both equal pay checks, and can be used for 'difficult' jobs that are more questionable using the main evaluation approach, eg jobs that are on the borderline between two grade definitions in a classification scheme. In other cases the analytical scheme is used more for external benchmarking reference – particularly where the outcomes tie in to a pay database.

Alternatives to formal analytical job evaluation

It must be assumed that not all organizations will be prepared to commit formally to using analytical job evaluation in conducting an equal pay review. Also, it is presumably the aim of equal pay legislation to reduce unfair and unjustifiable gender-based pay differences, not to impose a uniform approach to job evaluation and pay design in the UK. It is therefore important to identify a range of alternative tests that can contribute to a better understanding of whether the organization is paying equally for equal work.

Where analytical job evaluation is not used, there are other ways of comparing different types of jobs. These tests may not be as robust as applying analytical job evaluation across the organization but they can still be used to look for possible areas of pay discrimination. Some options for analysis are provided in Table 5.1.

The inescapable conclusion from these analysis options is that the more robust approaches incorporate job dimensions that are capable of being used to analyse different types of jobs on an organization-wide basis. This is, of course, the whole purpose of analytical job evaluation – whether or not it is used formally, it is the only way of being able to conduct robust comparisons across a range of different job types and functional specialisms.

CONCLUSION

The analysis options in Table 5.1 are particularly relevant to the step one gender pay gap analysis. They all enable organizations to identify where equal work is paid differently but this is by no means the end of the equal pay review process. Where this leads in terms of further analyses is amply covered in other sources of guidance.

As those organizations that have conducted equal pay reviews have found out, the potential causes of pay inequity are many and varied – there is the potential to get overwhelmed by the data requirements needed to carry out a comprehensive review. It is therefore important to prioritize effort, and to undertake those

Table 5.1 Comparing jobs without analytical job evaluation

Current approach to valuing jobs	Possible analyses
Whole-job approaches, eg discretionary, whole-job ranking, and paired comparison	Review what criteria are really being used – is it market, length of service, loyalty to the managing director, personal favouritism?

Take jobs at the same organization level or grade and compare the pay for men and women within each level. If there are no grades, use a simple categorization into organization levels, for example:

▌ director;
▌ senior manager responsible for a significant part of the organization;
▌ other managers/specialists;
▌ first-line supervisors/technicians/senior clerical;
▌ skilled clerical/operational;
▌ entry level clerical/operational.

Use these categories to compare pay for men and women at each level. A more thorough approach is to build some descriptive criteria into how jobs are placed into each level (ie a simple form of classification scheme).

If the organization has a standard approach to defining levels of skills or competence, this could be applied across the organization to help define levels. However, it is rare for an organization to apply such a standardized approach across all functional specialisms and organizational levels. It is more likely to be useful at lower organizational levels where more standard approaches to skill acquisition and qualifications (eg NVQs) are likely to apply.

An alternative approach is to undertake spot checks on jobs where there is perceived to be an equal pay risk. In order for jobs to be compared across different work areas, they need to be compared against a small number of common job dimensions, eg level of applied expertise, span of decision making, responsibility for resources and work environment, perhaps by categorizing jobs according to whether they are low, medium or high against each dimension (ie a simple form of factor comparison). This is sometimes called 'benchmarking'.

A sample of jobs could also be ranked by conducting paired comparison using similar job dimensions. The results of the paired comparison on each dimension can be added together to yield a job rank order. This rank order can be split into levels and a gender pay gap analysis conducted for each level. The stacking exercise described in Chapter 7 can be used for the same purpose.

Market-based structure Although market factors may be cited as a genuine material factor in an equal pay claim, there is no such thing as an automatic market defence. Each case has to be objectively justified. The following questions will help to determine whether a market-based pay system is robust and defensible from an equal pay perspective:

Is the market data drawn from a reliable survey source, rather than by word of mouth or recruitment agencies?
Is there more than one source of data for each job?
Are consistent data sources used in the same way across the whole organization?
If there are jobs that are predominantly occupied by females, is there confidence that the market data used for referencing those jobs do not contain any gender bias?
Can evidence be supplied that market differences are sufficient to cause recruitment difficulties if differential pay levels are applied?
If a pay range is placed around the market reference point, the criteria for moving employees through the range will need to be examined – as will the actual pay differences between employees covered by the same market rate.

Over-reliance on market rates can also make an organization insensitive to internal relativities. Therefore it is helpful to use one of the analyses described for whole jobs to get a more balanced view about the relationship between market rates and internal job relativities.

Factor comparison Factor comparison schemes can easily be adapted for more rigorous analysis by creating a simple points-scoring mechanism based on allocating points to levels within factors. As jobs have already been allocated to a factor level, no additional analysis is required other than to add up a total points score for each job. This can be used to confirm the grade for the job, if applicable, or if there are broad bands or no grades, jobs can be placed into organization levels by separating the ranking based on the points scores into levels.

A gender pay gap analysis can then be conducted on each level.

Job classification The first test is whether the classification definitions are non-gender biased and sufficiently robust to support a fair allocation of jobs.

Spot checks can be undertaken to confirm that jobs are evaluated fairly as for the whole-job approaches described above.

If the grade descriptions in the classification chart are defined in sub-headings, a sample of jobs could be evaluated using the sub-headings as factors, as for the factor comparison approach outlined above. A simple points scoring can again be used to calculate a total points score. This enables the organization to test whether the resulting rank order indicates a different hierarchy of jobs from that indicated by the current grade/band structure. If so, is there any risk that the difference in results is due to gender bias?

Jobs evaluated using this approach can also be split into levels defined by points score and an equal worth test conducted on each level.

Role matching

Where jobs are matched to generic role profiles it may be worth undertaking a spot check of jobs, as described in the whole-job approach, to confirm that jobs are being ranked at an appropriate level relative to jobs that have been matched against different generic descriptions

analyses that are most likely to throw light on whether any potential inequities exist.

It should be noted that where an organization satisfies itself through an equal pay review and continuing monitoring that there is no systematic pay discrimination, it is still possible to be subject to an equal pay claim. However, the likelihood of claims occurring should be reduced, and any claims that do occur are more likely to be one-offs rather than reflecting a wider problem.

Ultimately, the test of an equal pay review is whether the organization has reached evidence-based conclusions that it is systematically applying non-discriminatory criteria for determining pay and for achieving outcomes that are defensible and justifiable, or, if not, it knows what is needed to address any inequities. Looking for such evidence should be an ongoing responsibility of every organization to enable them to demonstrate that employees are being treated fairly. For this reason, the demand for robust, analytical approaches to valuing jobs will remain a constant organizational requirement.

References

1. EOC *Code of Practice on Equal Pay*, published initially in 1997 and updated in 2003

2. EOC *Equal Pay Review Kit*, 2002

3. *Equal Pay Guide*, published by the Chartered Institute of Personnel and Development, 2002

4. Kingsmill *Report on Women's Pay and Employment 2001*

6

Planning a new job evaluation scheme

OVERVIEW

This chapter, and the next, are intended to be a practical guide on how to develop a job evaluation scheme. They concentrate on developing an analytical points-factor scheme, as this illustrates the more demanding design issues. However, many of the design considerations apply equally well to the other types of job evaluation described in Chapter 2. The steps are:

1. identifying and defining the scheme factors;

2. analysing jobs;

3. testing the draft factor plan;

4. developing the scoring model;

5. preparing for implementation.

In practice, these steps are not always consecutive and some may need to be repeated in order to test and validate the scheme fully. Also, where a new pay structure is being implemented in conjunction with job evaluation, there are some parallel steps, as shown in Figure 6.1 which illustrates the design stages.

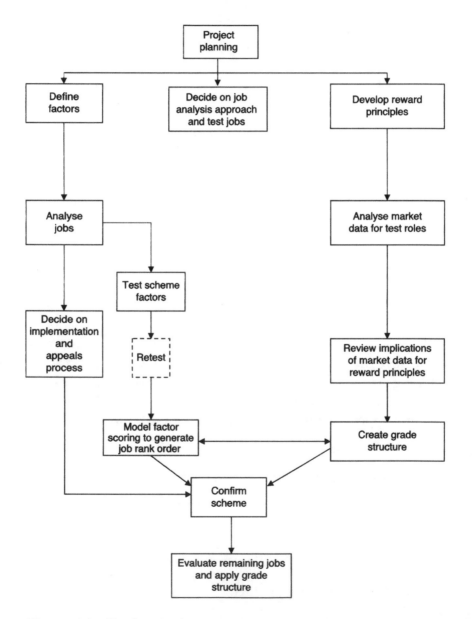

Figure 6.1 Design stages

Before embarking on scheme design, there are two preparatory steps that must be completed: 1) choosing the scheme design and 2) project planning. This chapter concentrates on these first two steps, with the next chapter focusing on the more technical aspects of scheme design.

CHOOSING A JOB EVALUATION SCHEME

Before embarking on detailed planning, it is necessary to have at least a preliminary view about what type of scheme will meet the organization's needs. This decision may be made by the project team that will work on the detailed scheme design. However, experience suggests that the decision is often made in advance by the human resources function or a reward strategy steering group in the light of the organization's broader human resources or reward strategy. If the decision on the type of scheme does not involve all of the relevant stakeholders, it is important to ensure that they are presented with, and are given the opportunity to discuss, the rationale for the type of scheme chosen, early on in the project.

Whoever is involved in the decision making will need to evaluate the options described in Chapter 2 against a set of criteria that are deemed important to the organization, for example:

- simplicity versus rigour;

- cost and time constraints;

- minimizing administration;

- the extent to which the organization is comfortable with, or wants to avoid, ongoing reliance on external support;

- whether computer support is needed;

- the extent to which a robust defence to potential equal pay claims is sought (around three-quarters of respondents to the E-Reward survey stated that equal value considerations were one of the reasons for having job evaluation);

▮ how job evaluation will be used to support equal pay reviews;

▮ what type of scheme is most likely to be supported internally by management and staff;

▮ the organization's history of job evaluation: one that has had a sophisticated points factor scheme in the past is likely to have a different perspective from one that has never had a job evaluation scheme;

▮ how the 'unique' characteristics of the organization will be taken into account;

▮ whether the organization wants to introduce a new way of describing jobs or recording job information;

▮ potential for links to other human resource policies.

Assuming that the decision is made to introduce a points factor scheme, the next decision relates to the extent to which the organization wants to tailor the scheme to meet their own needs. Schemes can be broadly split into three levels of customization:

1. proprietary schemes developed by consultants, applying standard factors and scoring models that have been tried and tested across a range of organizations or designed specifically for a sector;

2. customized schemes, based on an existing scheme, for example one developed by consultants, but that is capable of being adapted to address the organization's needs;

3. tailor-made schemes, developed entirely in-house or with the aid of an external adviser.

Based on the views expressed by the respondents to the E-Reward survey, the perceived pros and cons of each approach are summarized in Table 6.1.

Table 6.1 Pros and cons of different approaches to customization

Degree of customization	Benefits	Risks
Proprietary	▦ tried and tested, with an established reputation; ▦ the consultants can draw on extensive experience of implementing similar schemes; ▦ does not require intensive design effort; ▦ may link to pay database; ▦ computer support may be available as part of the package; ▦ consultancy may have international network for implementation;	▦ factors may suit some types of organization more than others; ▦ may not lead to high level of internal ownership; ▦ may be difficult to explain rationale for scoring and weighting; ▦ can lead to ongoing reliance on external provider; ▦ may include elements or supporting processes that do not meet organizational requirements, eg lengthy job descriptions.
Customized	▦ draws on external experience, so saves on design time; ▦ gives a starting point to the design process, but gives opportunities to engage employees.	▦ needs careful design input and implementation to avoid same risks as for proprietary scheme; ▦ need to avoid 'cherry picking' factors or scheme design elements that do not logically hang together.
Tailor-made	▦ reflects the values and language of the organization – focuses on what is important; ▦ fits the particular needs at the time; ▦ participative design process likely to lead to greater buy-in; ▦ no ongoing reliance on external provider; ▦ able to align to competency framework.	▦ needs investment of time and resources to develop scheme; ▦ unless expertise is available in-house, needs external support through development process.

Having made this decision, or at least narrowed down the options, the next step is to plan the project in detail. The need for disciplined project planning is emphasized by one respondent to the E-Reward survey, commenting that job evaluation 'should be run like a project with specific success criteria and... (do) not be afraid to amend it as appropriate rather than letting job evaluation run the organization'.

PROJECT PLANNING

A project plan will include all five technical design steps listed at the beginning of this chapter. However, an important aspect of project planning is to agree how stakeholders will be involved in the scheme design, and managing their perceptions. Getting this right is critical because there is overwhelming evidence that successful scheme implementation is determined as much by how it is perceived internally as in the minutiae of technical design details.

Project planning should therefore include:

▪ who will be covered by the scheme;

▪ who will be involved in the scheme development;

▪ resources – financial and people;

▪ how to monitor for equal value issues;

▪ the communications plan;

▪ the design timetable.

Who will be covered by the scheme?

Assuming that one of the main purposes of job evaluation is to help ensure equity of pay decisions, there is a strong argument for including all employees in the scheme. This gives less potential for pay discrimination than where employees are covered by a range of different evaluation or pay systems. But it may require a radical change in outlook by some of the stakeholders where different collective negotiating arrangements or pay structures have traditionally covered different employee groups. However, the E-Reward survey showed that nearly three-quarters of organizations now operate a single scheme.

If there are justifiable and non-discriminatory reasons for not including all employees in the scheme, consideration will need to be given to how read-across can be achieved across the employee groups inside and outside the scheme. This is needed in order to conduct equal pay reviews, which should span occupational boundaries.

Who will be involved in scheme development?

As with the introduction of any human resource initiative, evidence shows that broad involvement and consultation during scheme development increases scheme credibility and robustness, by ensuring that different perspectives are taken into account.

There are several stakeholder groups that will have an interest in the job evaluation design. These include top management, staff and trade unions or other employee representatives.

Unless a job evaluation study is being undertaken entirely as a background exercise, for example to support an equal pay review, implementing a job evaluation scheme invariably involves a project team to take the project through from design to implementation. Many organizations have their own project management processes and structures. Where there are none, a typical structure might include:

- Steering group: decisions about the development of the scheme will need to be made at key stages of the project. Depending on the size of the organization, it is helpful to have a steering group that speaks with the authority of the organization and that can ratify these key decisions. In a small organization the steering group may be the senior management team or directors. In comparison, schemes developed for an industry sector are more likely to include a balance of employer representatives and national trade union officials.

- Project sponsor at senior management level: their role is to provide a communications link to the management team, to provide a top-management perspective and knowledge, to ensure resources are made available, to be a sounding board and to give a steer on tactics and matters of principle.

- Project leader: accountable for the overall project management.

- Project administrator: to provide administrative support to the project. This is particularly helpful in large job evaluation projects where a lot of coordination is needed, for example in administering and tracking the job analysis process.

▌ Project team: to participate in the design process.

An integrated job evaluation and pay design project structure and roles for a building society, which encompasses job evaluation, pay structure design and the link between pay and performance management, is illustrated in Figure 6.2.

Careful consideration should be given to the selection of project team members. Selecting members who represent a diagonal slice across the organization by level and by function works well in offering different perspectives during scheme development. In addition, gender balance should be taken into account. As the EOC Good

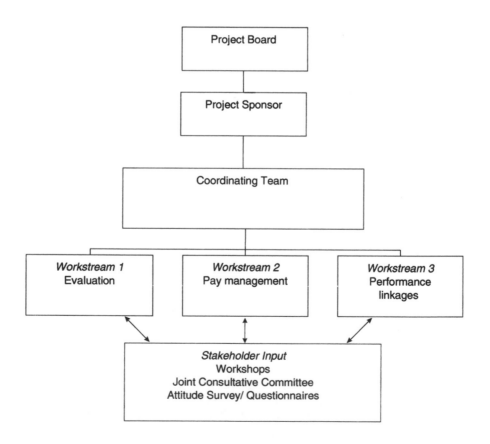

Figure 6.2 Building society job evaluation project structure

Practice Guide states, 'It is recognized good practice in job evaluation to include in these groups a representative sample of people from the spread of jobs covered by the scheme. A fair representation of women in all job evaluation groups and discussions is strongly recommended as a means of reducing the probability of sex bias.' Similarly, where an organization extends its monitoring beyond gender monitoring, consideration should be given to other areas of representation.

As well as ensuring broad representation, it is necessary to think about what kind of expertise will support the project. For example, a project team might include members with:

- specific organizational responsibility for equality or diversity;

- internal communications experience;

- knowledge of the organization's previous grading or job evaluation history;

- input from a quality management perspective;

- personnel knowledge;

- trade union or other formal employee representation.

If there are recognized trade unions, their representatives should be included in the project team as this is more likely to commit both parties to the outcome of the development process. Full union engagement is encouraged by the ACAS guidelines, which state that 'in the event of an equal value claim, a jointly agreed analytical scheme is more likely to be regarded as fair by an employment tribunal'. Many trade unions are willing to be involved 'without prejudice' in scheme development in a non-negotiating forum, often as full project team or steering group members, but they usually retain the formal right to negotiate on the scheme outcomes at the end of the process. Similarly, it can be helpful to involve members of an existing staff consultative forum where there is no formal trade union recognition.

The project team should have terms of reference that clarify the boundaries of the project and define their role. Typically, their role consists of:

- providing their ideas and input at all stages of the scheme design;

- being an advocate for the project;

- communicating with their colleagues;

- being a sounding board for the detailed design work that takes place outside the project team meetings.

The size of the project team will vary from one organization to the next. There is a balance between ensuring broad representation and keeping the team to a workable size. Experience suggests that teams of more than 10 people can be less effective in providing the scope for all team members to make an equal contribution. However, more than 10 may be needed to ensure full representation, for example in a unionized environment where several unions are represented and want to be involved. On the other hand, a team of less than six or seven is unlikely to be representative of the organization.

Finally, it is worth noting that project team members may feel daunted at the beginning of a project. However, many organizations find that as the project progresses their confidence increases, to the extent that by the end of the project individual team members are frequently keen to continue their involvement into full scheme implementation.

Resources

A decision needs to be made early on about what resources will be required to complete a job evaluation project. It is wise not to underestimate this. The largest financial outgoings are likely to be the cost of buying in external support and software, if needed. However, at least as important as the financial cost is the internal time commitment. It is particularly important for the project team members to be given an indication of the time they may have to spend on the project to ensure that they can commit to the demands of the project. The level of commitment needs to be made clear to all other interested parties, as the scheme design and testing may involve a large number of employees who are not part of the project team.

Account should also be taken of the extent to which there are any other major organizational initiatives under way. The possibility of a clash of priorities at key project stages needs to be identified so that this can be allowed for in the project plan.

Using external advisers

An early decision is whether to use an external resource. It may well be worth while getting support where in-house expertise is non-existent or limited. Many people are exposed to a new job evaluation scheme only once or twice in their careers, whereas a good external adviser will have experience of applying job evaluation schemes in many different settings, and can provide an in-depth knowledge of both technical design issues and the potential pitfalls around putting in a new scheme.

This will be particularly important if the intention is to use some form of computer-aided process for the continuing evaluation of jobs (see Chapter 8). The choice of which type of software (and which supplier) should be made very early on in the design phase. Knowing the input and other requirements of the software system in advance should minimize the work and time required to convert from the paper design to the computer process.

Support can come from a range of sources, including ACAS, employers' associations and consultants. In making a decision about which external adviser to use, consideration needs to be given to what role they will play. This can range from providing a packaged solution, as in a consultant's proprietary scheme, to facilitating the process that will help the organization develop its own scheme. The level of support can vary from providing hands-on input to acting as a sounding board to the development process.

The following checklist will help the decision about which consultant or adviser to use:

- How closely does the adviser's view of their role match the organization's own expectations?

- Depending on the degree of customization required, what is the adviser's experience in proprietary, customized or tailor-made schemes?

- How well does their experience relate to the organization/sector?

- To what extent does the prospective adviser focus on the technical aspects of scheme design, compared with the non-technical aspects?

- What is their level of familiarity with equal pay for work of equal value issues?

- What tests do they recommend as a matter of course to ensure that the scheme will not be biased?

- To what extent will the organization want to be dependent on the external adviser in the future?

- To what extent will the scheme be badged as the organization's own, or as the consultants' scheme?

- If the scheme is to be computer-aided, to what extent does the computer support the process? Can the provider guarantee good on-site and off-site support and training? Can they provide reference sites?

- How does the consultant charge for and record their fees? What happens if the scope of the project changes? Are they clear about how they charge for additional expenses, for example is there a standard loading for overheads? Do they charge separately for administrative/secretarial time? What is the licence or purchase fee for any software-related support and to what extent does this vary between stand-alone and networked versions?

▮ Last but not least, what is the fit? Does the consultant's style suit the organization? Bear in mind that the success of a project is related not only to the technical design of the scheme, but also to the organizational credibility of the scheme, which is obtained through communication, consultation and involvement; an external adviser can have a significant impact on the development and implementation process in this regard.

EQUAL VALUE CONSIDERATIONS

Testing the robustness of the scheme for equal pay issues is essential throughout the process, from scheme selection to implementation. The project plan needs to incorporate specific tests to ensure that the scheme is unbiased. These are summarized in Appendix 4. However, it is worth highlighting that at an early stage key stakeholders should receive training in equal value issues, including:

▮ the background to equal pay issues in the UK;

▮ the legislative framework;

▮ what tests need to be applied to scheme design and implementation to ensure that equal pay for equal value principles are followed.

The Equal Pay Act focuses solely on gender discrimination; however, in designing the scheme the potential for other types of discrimination, such as race and disability, should also be considered.

PLANNING COMMUNICATIONS

Putting in place a communications plan is an essential part of project planning. The credibility of a new job evaluation scheme rests on how effectively it is communicated. The most widely reported problem with job evaluation reported in the E-Reward survey was the lack of understanding of the scheme by managers and employees. The most common advice given to those who might be engaged in a job evaluation exercise by respondents to that survey is to communicate as much as possible.

The E-Reward survey respondents also stressed the importance of being specific about the business need for job evaluation. This needs to start at the beginning of the design process. Employees must understand the rationale and trust the design and implementation process. The same applies to the organization's leadership. As one HR manager said, 'the business leaders should have been involved more from the outset to ensure their buy-in'.

The project plan should allow for an early communication to cover the following points:

- Setting expectations: what is the intention behind bringing in a new job evaluation scheme? Perceptions about a scheme's introduction will depend on the culture and pay history of the organization. For example, there might be an expectation that this is an opportunity for everyone's pay to go up. Elsewhere, it may be the opposite. If there has been a recent reorganization, it may be necessary to address concerns about whether job evaluation is linked to further restructuring and redundancies. Another common perception that needs addressing early is the misconception that job evaluation is linked to measuring individual performance.

- Design principles – let staff know early decisions about scheme design.

- Any pay-related principles; for example, no one's pay will be reduced as a result of introducing the scheme.

- Any early decisions or principles on assimilation, for example a commitment to ensure that there will be a mechanism to avoid 'fossilizing' existing pay inequalities.

- Who is involved in scheme design, who project team members are and how they can be contacted.

The project plan needs to incorporate communications to staff at key points later in the project; for example, if job information needs to be collected from a broad sample of jobs, communication is needed to explain the process and reassure both those who will be involved in the process and those who are not.

There are key stages in a job evaluation project when communication is essential: as the project starts, before employees are involved in job analysis, when the scheme design is complete and when the new pay structure is attached to the scheme. Here are examples of what some organizations have done to make their communications more effective throughout the process:

▋ provide a telephone help line number, using an answer-phone to collect questions;

▋ give out contact numbers and e-mail addresses of all project team members;

▋ create distinctive project communications; for example, special bulletins on coloured paper;

▋ put information on the intranet;

▋ brief staff regularly through team meetings, directors' meetings and any other regular communications briefings;

▋ run informal lunchtime sessions so that staff can ask questions about any aspect of scheme design and implementation – tie these in to take place shortly after written communications;

▋ use organizational knowledge on identifying the most effective way to reach all staff; for example, some organizations attach information bulletins to pay slips as the only guaranteed way of reaching all staff;

▋ use a range of media, to take account of the fact that different people receive and absorb communications messages in different ways (visual, auditory, written).

The experience of organizations that have gone through this process is that it is best to avoid giving definite completion dates if there is any chance that the timetable might deviate from the original plan.

It is necessary to manage expectations carefully by communicating only those dates that are known to be achievable, and to be clear about what will, and will not, be achieved by then. A date is the one thing that everyone remembers. If a communication states that the scheme design will be completed by 1 May, employees will expect the scheme to be implemented and all jobs evaluated by that date, even if implementation is planned to follow on later.

THE DESIGN TIMETABLE

Having taken account of all the above factors, it is worth stopping to confirm whether now is the right time to be conducting a job evaluation project. For example, is restructuring likely in the near future? If so, will the job evaluation scheme support the allocation of jobs to the new structure, or will it be better to get the restructuring out of the way, and to evaluate jobs in the new structure once it has settled into place?

With respect to planning the detailed timing, it is usually possible to predict the amount of time required for the technical aspects of scheme design. Variation in the timetable is more likely to be the result of:

- the level and type of involvement and consultation that is needed to ensure that the scheme will be acceptable and credible;

- the extent to which the scheme is likely to need more than one iteration of testing;

- whether there are plans to pilot the scheme in one part of the organization prior to full implementation;

- the approach that will be taken to job analysis, including whether good quality job information is already available about all the jobs to be evaluated or whether it will be necessary to analyse jobs afresh to meet job evaluation needs;

- the decision-making process in the organization: for example, if key decisions are made by a senior-level committee that meets once a month or quarter, the project plan will need to tie in with this meeting schedule.

For these reasons, project timetables can vary significantly. At the simplest level a project involves three main tasks:

1. Decide on overall scheme design.

2. Agree and test scheme factors and scoring.

3. Evaluate jobs.

However, this process and the amount of work involved vary immensely depending on the size and complexity of the organization. For a simple scheme the design could be completed in only two to three months. However, a more typical project plan would extend to six to nine months, and in a large organization or federation of organizations the design may take up to twelve months.

Completion through to full implementation is even more variable as it depends on whether to evaluate all the remaining jobs that have not been part of the development process. The alternative is to evaluate a representative group of jobs (benchmarks), with the remaining jobs being matched to grades, based either on their closeness of fit to these benchmark jobs or to a summary description of the grading criteria for that grade based on the jobs that have already been evaluated into each grade (classification).

Finally, it is advisable to build some flexibility into the project plan. It should be assumed that the first attempt at scheme design will not be perfect. There may be a need for additional design work or testing, and this should be allowed for.

Whatever the size and scope of the project, the plan should cover the following:

▓ key stages;

▓ deliverables from each stage;

▓ dates and milestones;

▓ responsibility for delivering each item in the plan.

An outline project plan used by a financial services institution is illustrated in Figure 6.3.

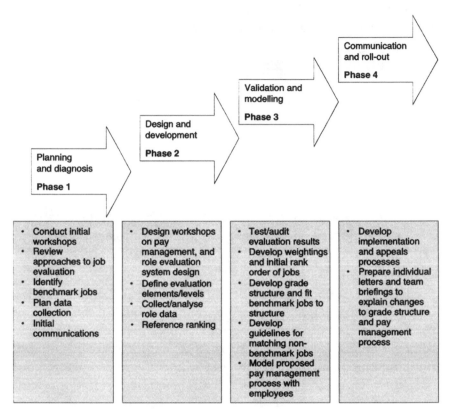

Figure 6.3 Project phases

7

Scheme design

The most common type of job evaluation is points-factor rating as described in Chapter 2. The E-Reward survey found that 63 per cent of respondents with job evaluation schemes used this approach. Two important reasons for its popularity are, first, because as an analytical process it provides evaluators with defined yardsticks which help them to achieve a reasonable degree of objectivity and consistency in making their judgements, and second, because it facilitates the achievement of equal pay for work of equal value and provides a defence in an equal value case as long as it is not discriminatory in itself.

This chapter therefore concentrates on the design of points-factor schemes. It covers the five steps that need to be taken to design such schemes, namely:

1. identify and define factors to produce draft factor plan;

2. analyse jobs;

3. test the draft factor plan;

4. develop the scoring model, ie the weighting and scoring progression;

5. prepare for implementation.

IDENTIFYING AND DEFINING FACTORS

Factors are the primary means of communicating the values of an organization and the elements of a job that deserve recognition. (IDS[1])

As described in Chapter 2, job evaluation factors are the characteristics or key elements of jobs that are used to analyse jobs in an analytical job evaluation scheme. The factors must be capable of identifying relevant and important differences between jobs that will support the creation of a ranking of the jobs to be covered by the scheme. They should apply equally well to different types of work, including specialists and generalists, lower-level and higher-level jobs, and not be biased in favour of one gender or group. Although many of the job evaluation factors used across organizations capture similar job elements, the task of identifying factors can be challenging.

There are a number of different approaches to identifying factors. Whatever approach is used, the final tests are that they:

▌ are seen as important and acceptable criteria for creating pay differences between jobs;

▌ describe the same characteristic or element at different levels in order to differentiate meaningfully between jobs;

▌ are understandable and written in a way that is meaningful to those who will be covered by the scheme;

▌ are comprehensive, but avoid double counting;

▌ are acceptable to those who will be covered by the scheme;

▌ are not biased.

If the above tests are met, a simple scheme with relatively few factors can meet organizational requirements as much as a more sophisticated scheme. As stated in the ACAS job evaluation guidance notes,[2] 'simple job evaluation techniques acceptable to both parties can be just as effective as complex ones'. The advice from respondents to the E-Reward survey[3] was also to keep it simple. In practice, however, larger, more complex organizations typically include more factors to ensure that the scheme is balanced and fair to all the employee groups covered by the scheme. For example, the scheme developed for the National Health Service has 16 factors, the local government NJC scheme has 13 and the scheme developed for further education has 11 factors with a total of 23 sub-factors.

Sources of information

The following sources of information and approaches to support the development of factors are available:

▌ *Reviewing internal strategy/business documents*: looking through existing written materials such as organization or human resources strategy documents can give an insight into the current values and language.

▌ *Reviewing people-related frameworks or processes*: in the past, job evaluation criteria were not necessarily linked to other human resources processes or frameworks; however, many organizations have now accepted the need to have a more coherent approach by applying the organization's values and language across related processes. Reviewing existing job descriptions may be a place to start. However, the most obvious potential link is with an organization's competency framework, as many of the concepts reflected in competencies are similar to job evaluation criteria, albeit expressed in behavioural or skills-based language. How closely a link can be made with an existing competency framework will, of course, depend on how the competency framework has been defined. However, the desirability of achieving a degree of linkage was a finding from the E-Reward survey, and was one of the main reasons for companies favouring a tailor-made scheme.

▮ *Interviews with line managers and other stakeholders:* discussions with key managers can help to get an early perspective on the senior management priorities for the scheme. This group is most likely to have a view about the future demands on the organization and what work will be valued. Early senior manager involvement can also help to dispel myths and misconceptions about job evaluation, and can support the overall communications process – particularly if the managers concerned are those who will later be responsible for approving the scheme.

▮ *Focus groups:* structured meetings with employees can be an effective way of understanding what aspects of jobs are currently valued, and what people think should be of most importance. The process can also provide a positive contribution to the overall involvement and communications process. As employees may be unfamiliar with job evaluation concepts, the agenda will normally need to cover: an overview of what job evaluation is, the rationale for introducing job evaluation, what factors are and what makes a 'good' factor. Then views can be explored on possible factors. Focus groups can also be used to explore employee views about how the scheme should be communicated further.

Focus groups can be particularly useful for organizations with geographically or functionally diverse constituencies or for developing sector-wide schemes. In developing the further education scheme, focus groups were run in about a dozen colleges around the country. They were selected to represent different types of institution as well as geographic diversity. The focus groups generated a long list of possible factor headings, which showed a high degree of consistency across the institutions. This input was clustered into 11 main groups, which became the factors.

Consideration should also be given as to whether to get input from other stakeholders. For example, a voluntary organization may want to involve volunteers in focus groups, or to solicit the views of key trustees. But this is unusual. It is more common and necessary to involve trade unions or other employee representatives at an early stage.

▓ *Project team input:* the project team can explore possible factors in a number of ways, for example:

– Open discussion – drawing on the inputs that are available to the team from other sources.

– Selecting a number of jobs/roles and exploring the differences between them – what makes one 'bigger' or 'smaller' than another. This can be done informally or through a process such as whole-job ranking or paired comparison. Another exercise that can be used for the same purpose is 'stacking'. This process involves putting job titles on cards, and splitting the cards into ever-smaller groups, discussing and documenting the criteria as the decisions on group allocation are made (see illustration of process in Appendix 5).

– Using an existing database or list of common factor headings; posting these up on a flipchart and drawing out and clustering the job dimensions that seem most relevant to the organization. If a consultant is being used, this exercise is likely to use headings from their factor database.

Job evaluation factor headings

When the main job dimensions have been identified, they need to be sorted into clusters, for the purpose of identifying the main factor headings. An analysis of job evaluation factors show that they typically fall into six main areas:

1. the combination of the skills, knowledge or experience that the employee needs to do the job;

2. the thinking challenges of the job, for example planning, analysis, decision making and problem solving;

3. interpersonal skills, including communication and relationship building skills;

4. the responsibilities that the job has for resources, eg human, financial or physical resources;

5. the kinds of impact that the role has, either on internal operational effectiveness or on the external customer or environment;

6. the environmental, emotional or physical demands that are made in a job, for example difficult working conditions, involvement in dealing with challenging behaviour or operational dexterity.

Within these six areas there are many different ways in which jobs can be described. This will depend on the extent to which the organization wants to express jobs in terms of responsibility or the effects of the job on the organization, or in terms of the 'inputs' that a job requires, ie what combination of applied knowledge, skills or behaviours (ie competencies). For example, most organizations include a factor relating to communication skills in their scheme. However, one organization may define this as the interpersonal skills needed to build relationships; another might place emphasis on the level and type of internal or external contacts that the job is required to have; yet another might focus on core verbal and aural communication skills required at different levels. Factors are a vehicle for communicating values – what is important to the organization, so there is no 'right' answer to factor selection, subject to reasonableness tests discussed later in the chapter. Appendix 6 provides a matrix of factors used by participants in the E-Reward survey, separated into 'skills and behaviours' and 'responsibilities and effects' headings. Appendix 8b lists the factors contained in the scheme developed by the writers of this book for the Association of Colleges (further education).

To ensure that the scheme is fair across the whole employee population, it is important to identify factors that are balanced across the population. If the scheme includes a factor that is oriented towards one type of job, it needs to be counterbalanced by factors that are relevant for other staff. A charity specializing in providing community care included a factor about responsibility for caring for others, while balancing this with factors relating to responsibility for resources and for staff. From an equality perspective this balance is particularly important if any factors are more likely to relate to one gender. In a company that tended to employ male warehouse operators and female clerical staff, a working conditions factor and an operational dexterity factor were included.

Sub-factors

Some points factor schemes break down broad factor categories into sub-factors. For example, if an organization decides to include a factor or factors relating to 'Impact', ie the internal operational and external impact of jobs, there are a number of ways of capturing this:

1. a single factor that encapsulates both the internal and external aspects of impact;

2. one factor for internal impact and a separate factor for external impact, recognizing that while some jobs have an internal focus and impact, others have an external focus, and some have both;

3. one factor called 'Impact' containing two sub-factors, one relating to internal and one relating to external impact.

It could be argued that there is no difference between points 2 and 3. However, the difference between the two is more likely to be apparent when points are attached to each of the factors. A decision on how to cluster factors and whether to have sub-factors may well anticipate how the scheme will be scored: whether a separate internal and external 'impact' factor are each considered to be as important as other factors, or whether a single 'impact' factor made up of two sub-factors is more likely to have a similar weighting to the other main factor headings.

This decision might also be steered by how simple or complex the organization wants the scheme to be. Does the organization want a simple scheme that is capable of being administered on a simple spreadsheet or is it prepared to support greater sophistication?

Developing the factors

In developing the factors, a logical sequence is first to define and get agreement within the project team (and with the steering group if there is one) on what each of the factor headings should be, including a brief explanation of what falls under the heading, before embarking on the longer process of defining factor levels. It is important to get this initial definition right, as it will determine the scope of each factor and allow checks to be made on the completeness and balance of the factors, as well as ensuring that double counting is avoided.

Identifying and defining levels

When the factor headings and definition have been agreed, the next step is to identify and define levels for each factor. It would be a frustrating and impractical task for the detailed drafting to be done by the project team. This is a task that is better delegated to one or two team members; if a consultant is being employed, this is often a task that they will take on.

However, before the drafting starts, it is helpful to have team input on possible factor levels. The project team can be asked to brainstorm examples of what would characterize the highest or lowest level for each factor, based on what they know about jobs in the organization. To do this thoroughly in a limited time, the team can work in small groups, with each group working on different factors; each small team can then circulate their work on to another team when they have finished, and so on until each team has had a chance to review and add to the ideas put down for each factor. This is the approach adopted for developing the NHS JES factor levels. This process led to review of some of the initially selected factors, as it became clear that there was double counting.

Initial factor testing

When an initial draft of the factors has been prepared, this needs to be tested. This first stage of testing involves checking:

1. Whether any important dimensions of jobs are missing; particular care should be taken to ensure a balance between the

types of work primarily performed by both male and female employees.

2. Whether the language is clear, and likely to be understandable across the organization: for example, if relative terms like 'small', 'medium' and 'large' have been used, are they able to be interpreted consistently across the organization? If not, should they be changed or will there need to be supplementary guidance notes?

3. Whether the steps between levels in each factor or sub-factor describe measurable steps and whether the number of levels seems right.

4. Whether each of the factors captures a distinct and separate job dimension, rather than compressing two or more concepts into the same factor; for example, if thinking skills are captured in the scheme, does the requirement for analysing issues need to be captured separately from the need to come up with solutions, or can they be encompassed in the same factor?

5. That the factors do not double count each other; for example, factors such as decision making and freedom to act or autonomy may well contain overlap – if so, are both factors necessary?

6. Whether there is a balance between simplicity and thoroughness; factor wording problems reported by organizations with job evaluation schemes in the E-Reward survey included, on the one hand, problems relating to insufficient detail and over-generalization and, on the other, overly prescriptive wording.

There are several different ways to do this first stage testing, for example by:

▌ getting project team members to read through and comment on the factor level definitions before or during a project team meeting;

▌ presenting small groups of project team members with sets of factors that have been cut up and reordered, with the request that they recompile each factor into the same order that they think they were drafted in; this is a very effective exercise in making all participants review both the wording and sense of individual phrases, as well as in testing the clarity of the level definitions;

▌ the project team using the draft on a small number of test jobs; this testing might be on 'dummy' jobs, on a small number of pre-prepared jobs, or on a sample of jobs that the team members are familiar with.

The next stage of testing is to take the draft factor plan beyond the project team, and into the organization. How this is done will depend on the decision that is taken on how jobs will be analysed. This is described in detail below.

ANALYSING JOBS

One of the early decisions in introducing a new job evaluation scheme will be about the job information that will be needed in order to evaluate jobs. This decision is often tied up with the initial choice of scheme design, and affects the initial and ongoing resource requirements for scheme development. The decision needs to be linked to the range of purposes to which the job analysis information might be put, as it can provide data for a range of key personnel processes, including organization design, job design, human resource planning, recruitment, performance management, and training and development.

The main alternatives are described below.

Job descriptions

The traditional view of job evaluation is that it needs to be supported by job descriptions written to a format that matches the factor definitions. Typically, job descriptions contain an overview of the job and its place in the organization structure, detailed descriptions of duties and responsibilities and commentary tailored to each of the job evaluation scheme's factor headings. In some organizations job analysts' careers have been built on compiling and crafting such documents. Similarly, many line managers are well versed in the art of generating job descriptions to meet the needs of their job evaluation scheme, in order to create a new job or regrade an existing job.

It is undeniable that many schemes continue to be supported by job descriptions. In some cases this is because the organization already has job descriptions in place, and wants to use these as a basis for evaluation. If so, these need to be looked at to see whether their existing format is sufficiently robust to meet the needs of the scheme that is being developed, or whether they need to be updated or written in a new format.

Case study: a small charity was planning to introduce a new job evaluation scheme but had recently gone through the process of rewriting job descriptions. Although the job descriptions were not tailored to meet the factors subsequently developed for the job evaluation scheme, a decision was taken that the combination of job description information and the existing job knowledge of the cross-functional project team would be sufficient to enable most jobs to be evaluated. The project team members evaluated each of the 30 or so jobs individually using the job descriptions, then brought together their results for group discussion. Additional job information was sought only where project team members felt that the job description information and the team's job knowledge were insufficient to evaluate the job. In practice, this affected only a small number of the 30 or so jobs that were evaluated.

Where job descriptions are used as a foundation for job evaluation, the information contained in the job description has to be converted into job evaluation outcomes, ie a decision has to be made on what level definition best fits the job for each factor. This is typically done either by the project team evaluating a job together on the basis of the job description prepared by a trained analyst, or by the trained analyst evaluating the job, with the outcomes being reviewed in a team meeting.

Because robust information is an essential element in the achievement of effective job evaluation, many organizations have moved on from using lengthy job descriptions to better means of capturing the relevant job information.

Role profiles

Some organizations take the opportunity presented by a job evaluation exercise to redefine the way that work is described, switching away from a detailed job description to a role profile that focuses on the required skills, behaviours and outcomes or deliverables of the role, rather than on the detailed tasks that must be performed. As discussed in Chapter 1, the concept of a 'role' rather than 'job' focuses on what is needed to deliver organizational objectives, by setting out the behavioural expectations as well as the expected outcomes, rather than the minutiae of how the work needs to be done. The aim is to give more career development opportunity to employees in the role by focusing on the delivery of outcomes rather than how they get there. It also gives organizational flexibility by not detailing working methods and tools. Two examples of role profile format are given in Appendix 7.

Role profiles have the advantage of being more enduring documents than job descriptions as they do not need amending each time the detailed duties of the role change. Neither do they require the level of detail found in some job descriptions, as they are not so task focused. Changes in technology or organization do not have so much of an impact on broadly defined role responsibilities. For these reasons, it is possible to generate generic role profiles that capture information on a number of roles that might previously have been described using separate job descriptions. For example, one vehicle leasing company reduced over 180 job descriptions to just over 50 role profiles. However, in deciding on the use of generic role profiles it is necessary to consider the extent to which they might be used to support the broader range of personnel processes mentioned at the beginning of this section. For example, if role profiles are too generic they may not be suitable for recruitment purposes unless further information is obtained.

If role profiles are to be used to support job evaluation, they must be sufficiently descriptive to enable job evaluation decisions to be made. However, largely because of the introduction of computer-aided job evaluation, less reliance is now being placed on written job descriptions or role profiles.

Written questionnaire

Encouraged by the introduction of computer-aided job evaluation schemes, questionnaires based on the factor level definitions are now used as the source of evaluation information for some schemes.

Questionnaires can be given to the jobholders, or to jobholders and their managers, to complete. They may be administered directly to employees as a paper-based exercise on the basis that they know best how the job is done. However, the risk of giving the questionnaire directly to jobholders is that individuals tend to focus on their own role and can find it difficult to think about their role relative to others in the organization. This can lead to misleading patterns of responses, depending on the perceived importance of the role – it allows individuals to 'talk up' or downplay their roles. From an equal value perspective, this gives rise to concern as there is, at least, anecdotal evidence that men are more likely to talk up their roles than women. As a result, the process needed subsequently to validate self-completed questionnaires can be a long one.

Alternatively, questionnaires can be used as the basis for a structured interview with jobholders – either directly sharing the questionnaire with the jobholders, or using a structured interview guide, with the job analysts then evaluating the job against the factor definitions after the interview. Sharing a questionnaire with jobholders makes the scheme more transparent to the jobholder, if it is a multiple choice questionnaire and the employee has a direct input to evaluating the factor levels for their job. On the one hand, such transparency is advantageous, but on the other it is also conducive to employees talking up their job as they can see what is needed to get them to the highest levels in each factor. The use of trained job analysts reduces this risk as they can ask questions to elicit examples that help to pinpoint the appropriate level. However, this has the effect of reducing transparency as it requires the translation of the interviewee's responses, unless the evaluation is done with the active input of the jobholder.

As reported by IDS,[4] an approach used by the Biotechnology and Biological Sciences Research Council required jobholders and/or line managers to provide a summary of the job characteristics on a job assessment sheet which then formed the basis for an interview with a trained evaluator. This information was used to prepare a report on the job, which was agreed with the jobholder and line manager as a fair basis on which to make an evaluation. The evaluation was completed by the analyst using a multiple choice questionnaire based on the factor level definitions. The Ecclesiastical Insurance Group used trained analysts to administer a questionnaire to employees using a mix of different styles of questions on the factors which were dispersed throughout the questionnaire, to prevent employees honing in on the 'right' answer for each factor.

Computer-aided interview

Advanced computer-aided approaches such as the Gauge software provided by Pilat (Chapter 8) involve the jobholder, manager and job analyst sitting together around a PC to complete a set of online questions. This enables a more sophisticated questioning approach, whereby jobholders are asked questions that relate directly to their job, rather than all the questions embedded in the scheme. If the same initial question on a factor is answered differently, the next question that appears will be different. Again, this approach does not rely on job descriptions. An output of the interview is likely to be some form of job profile, based on the interviewee's answer.

However, where the final scheme will be computer-aided, it is likely that the initial scheme development will use a more traditional questionnaire approach in order to test the factors, before building these into the computer tool. This avoids regular and potentially expensive reconfiguration of the tool every time a change is made to the scheme.

Who will be moved?

Whichever approach to job analysis is used in the initial testing, a key decision is who will be involved in the job analysis process and when. This may include any combination of the following stakeholders:

▌ *the jobholder*, who knows how the job is done in practice;

▌ *the jobholder's manager*, who should have an overview of what is required of the job holder;

▌ *the manager's manager*, who may be used in a signing-off capacity or to resolve any differences between the jobholder and his or her manager;

▌ *a trained job analyst*, who can facilitate discussions between the jobholder and line manager, and help to resolve differences; analysts may be drawn from the project team, the HR function or a broader group of trained employees;

▌ *trade union representatives*, who may be involved as observers to the job analysis process, or sit in on interviews if requested by the jobholder(s).

The process used for job analysis and who is involved in it will determine how the job analysis information is turned into a set of evaluation responses that can be used in testing the factors.

Whoever is involved in the initial testing will need to be trained. This should cover:

▌ guidance on how to conduct interviews;

▌ guidance on how to apply the tool being used for collecting job information;

▌ awareness training on how to avoid discrimination;

▌ distinguishing between individual performance and the job requirements.

It is advisable to allow around an hour and a half to two hours for employee interviews. However, there will always be exceptions; in one organization interviews were typically taking around three hours. Although this is exceptional, when allocating resources it is advisable to plan for no more than two to three interviews a day.

TESTING THE DRAFT FACTOR PLAN

As well as deciding on the process for analysing jobs, it is necessary to decide which sample of jobs to test the factors on.

The factors should be tested on a representative sample of jobs. Test jobs will also be needed later in the design process to model the scoring of the scheme and to make the links between points and grades. A good time for deciding which test jobs to use is while the factors are being developed.

It is helpful to decide early on whether to use the same jobs for testing the factors as for the later testing. A common approach is for the factors to be tested initially on a smaller sample of jobs, with a broader sample being used later to test any factor amendments, to model the scheme scoring and to create a rank order of jobs that can be used to develop a grade structure. The decision may depend on the availability of job information, and on the approach to and timing of the job analysis process.

In a small organization the scheme might be developed using all the roles. However, it is usually more practicable to choose a sample of roles that are representative of the organization. This can be done by selecting a 'diagonal slice' of jobs covering all levels of job and the major functions or specialisms.

The process of identifying test roles is sometimes the first time that an organization has to get to grips with the number of distinct jobs they have. It is not unusual for organizations to find that they have more titles than jobs or roles, simply because a title may have been created for an employee for historical or status reasons; for example, a 'senior administrator' who does exactly the same as an 'administrator' who has three years' less service. Similarly, the titles may reflect sex bias: 'there is a long history of using different work titles for the jobs of men and women who are doing essentially the same work' (EOC[5]). This means that the first step in choosing test jobs may be to conduct an initial job title review to understand what jobs really exist. This can be used as an opportunity to rationalize job titles.

At the other extreme, organizations with broad banding may have swung in the opposite direction, resulting in broad title headings covering a multitude of jobs. Where this is the case, it may be necessary to recognize finer descriptions for testing purposes.

In choosing test jobs, the following points should also be considered:

- The list of jobs should be reviewed to ensure that it is representative of both genders, including some jobs that cover both sexes and some that are dominated by one sex.

- In order to make the test roles as representative of as large a part of the organization as possible, it is helpful to select roles that have a large number of incumbents, but it may also be useful to include some small-population jobs, where they have unique features (eg three sewing machinists at a specialist motor firm).

- It is not necessary to include roles from every job level or grade; however, by careful selection it is possible to select a group of roles that covers a large proportion of the organization's employees. This is helpful later for costing purposes, if a new grade structure is to be developed using the test roles.

- It helps if the test jobs/roles are well-established roles in the organization that are unlikely to change significantly. It is best to avoid highly controversial or unique roles, unless they are likely to test an aspect of the scheme that cannot otherwise be tested. Similarly, the jobs should be ones that actually exist rather than planned roles, as new roles sometimes evolve in ways that are not anticipated.

- If the scheme is going to have a close link to the external market, it helps to choose jobs/roles that can be readily benchmarked against market data.

▌ If a new grade structure is being introduced, the number of test jobs will ultimately need to be enough to enable decisions to be made on where the grades should be drawn across the rank order of roles. This will depend on how many grades the organization envisages having – the larger the number of planned grades, the more test jobs will be needed to establish robust grade boundaries. Fewer than around five or six roles for each planned grade are unlikely to be enough to make such decisions; more roles will be needed for complex organizations with many job families or functions.

▌ If the scheme is not covering the entire organization, jobs should be included that overlap with other plans either vertically or horizontally across the organization's structure, in order to support comparability exercises and equal pay reviews.

▌ Finally, an important consideration is whether these test roles will be used purely for scheme development or whether they will be used as anchors or reference jobs once the scheme is in place, in which case they are usually referred to as 'benchmark' jobs. If this is the intention, it is particularly important to select jobs that are not likely to change quickly.

In organizing the job analysis process it is also necessary to consider how to deal with multiple incumbent jobs. It may be appropriate to interview a number of incumbents in order to provide representative information. For example, this can be done by interviewing jobholders as a group or through separate interviews with a range of jobholders.

It may be desirable to test whether, in fact, all of the jobs occupied by incumbents with the same job title are indeed the same job – if so, it is useful to select incumbents that represent different ends of the spectrum in terms of the way in which the job is structured or the tasks that fall within it.

Validating factor definitions

The outcome of the job analysis process will be a factor-by-factor evaluation of the test jobs (further guidance on how this can be carried out is provided in Chapter 10). This information will be used to validate the factors. Validation can be achieved through statistical tests as well as by applying judgement to the findings. The project team will need to meet to review the initial set of results together. It saves time if this data is reviewed in advance to eliminate simple errors, such as missing data. If a computer-aided approach is being used, additional data tests may be available.

One way of reviewing the factors is to conduct a job-by-job review. Indeed, this represents the traditional 'panel' approach to evaluating jobs – with each job being analysed separately in turn against the draft factor definitions. However, an analytical approach that can be used both at this stage and when the scheme is fully implemented is a factor-by-factor review. This enables an in-depth review of each factor and, by focusing on factor results rather than the 'job', it can limit the impact of evaluator preconceptions about jobs. It also has the advantage over a job-by-job review that it tends to take less time, as it is possible to focus mainly on the jobs that are questionable relative to the levels allocated to all the other jobs.

If a factor-by-factor approach is used, the evaluation results are typically presented in rank order by level within each factor. This data can then be used to analyse:

▎ Whether factors are double counting each other – can any factors be combined, or one eliminated?

▎ Whether each of the levels in the factors is being used. If not, has the factor level been poorly worded? Is it redundant? Or has the sample of jobs chosen for this initial testing not been adequate to cover the level concerned?

▎ Whether the results of the initial factor analysis are heavily skewed. For example, are nearly all of the jobs covered by the lowest levels of the factor? If so, are the factor levels described appropriately to differentiate effectively between jobs? An example of a factor that was found to be skewed like this was in a public sector organization that wanted to include a health and safety factor due to an organizational priority on public safety. The first test revealed that very few jobs in the organization had more than the basic statutory responsibility, so it did not prove to be an effective differentiator for more than a few jobs, and was therefore abandoned as a factor.

▓ Whether the results look right on a 'felt-fair' basis. In some cases, apparent anomalies might be due to different job analysts applying a different interpretation of the level definitions. Where this is so, the factor level definitions may need to be clarified. Alternatively, some project teams find that there are 'rogue' analysts that consistently apply higher or lower levels than other analysts, particularly at the early stages of a job evaluation project. Evaluator differences can be tested if more than one job analyst has analysed the same job. However, the fact that a job might have a lower or higher level allocated to it than expected does not mean that it has been wrongly evaluated. In fact, if a new job evaluation scheme is to do any more than to reinforce the status quo, it is only to be expected that the job evaluation process may overturn some preconceptions about the existing job hierarchy.

By this stage it may be helpful to test any beliefs about whether the previous job ranking was biased by gender, so results can be analysed by gender, if gender data has been collected. If there have been concerns that the existing grade or pay structure is discriminatory, the results can be reviewed to see if the scheme is likely to address these issues.

At the end of this review the project team should have agreed which factors need amending. Also, depending on the extent to which the initial jobs are to be included in later testing on scoring the scheme, a decision needs to be made on whether to go back to jobholders to revalidate any of the levels due to changes agreed by the team, or whether to do some additional testing on a further sample of jobs. The test should also have yielded some important information about what procedures to use in fully implementing the scheme.

DECIDING ON FACTOR WEIGHTING AND THE SCORING MODEL

The outcome of points-factor evaluation is a ranking of roles (see Chapter 2), based on the total points score for each job. This section focuses on the decisions to be made about how factors should be weighted and the progression of points within factors (the scoring model).

The total points score will be influenced by the weighting given to each of the factors as determined by the maximum number of points attributed to each factor and the points progression within them. Factor weighting is expressed as the maximum points available for that factor taken as a percentage of the total available points for all factors. It can be 'explicit', ie different factors may have different scores, or 'implicit' as described below.

Weighting

There is no single 'right' approach to developing factor weights. The main approaches are:

▌ Using the pre-determined weighting built into a proprietary scheme.

▌ Statistical analyses; typically, this refers to multiple linear regression analysis that is used to predict what the 'best' combination of weights will be to replicate a reference ranking; less commonly, it involves analysing stakeholder views to tease out the most important factors. This form of analysis is described in more detail in Chapter 8.

▌ Applying judgement, which may involve open discussion or is based on agreed guiding principles (eg no factor will have a weighting of less than 5 per cent or more than 30 per cent).

▌ 'Implicit weighting', which means using the scoring progression that is implicit in the factor design, based on the number of factors and the number of levels in each factor. Thus, a simple scheme that has seven factors with four levels in each factor would yield a maximum score of 28 points if each factor level scores 1 point. Sometimes this is referred to as an unweighted scheme, but this is not the case because decisions on the number of factors and levels within them and the scoring progression used may in effect 'weight' the scheme. For example, in a seven-factor scheme with the same pattern of score progression per level in each factor but with two factors with more levels than the others, the factors with more levels will have been weighted.

The benefits and risks of the various approaches are summarized in Table 7.1.

Table 7.1 Comparison of approaches to weighting

Approach	Benefits	Risks
Consultancy developed	▌ tried and tested across many organizations; ▌ enables comparability across organizations.	▌ may place value on factors that are different from the organization's own values; ▌ may be perceived as a 'black box' approach if not understood internally; ▌ lack of transparency and ownership; ▌ possible challenge on equal value grounds;
Statistical analyses	▌ can be useful kick-start to the decision-making process; appears to be 'objective'.	▌ can yield unhelpful results, eg negative coefficients for factors that are most applicable to lower-level jobs; ▌ has an equal value risk because it relies on potentially biased reference ranking; ▌ may be difficult to know when to stop.
Judgemental	▌ reflects the values of the organization; ▌ can be as simple or complex as required to meet needs.	▌ can be unfocused if there are no guiding principles; ▌ may end up biased in favour of one group if the process turns into a negotiation, eg in one international development bank, the weighting debate became a negotiation between the economists, who argued for a high weighting on knowledge and expertise, and the investment bankers, who argued for the highest weighting on financial impact.
Implicit	▌ easy to understand; ▌ easy to calculate; ▌ avoids protracted discussions about weighting, which may only marginally affect the overall rank order.	▌ may not reflect relative importance of a factor that is particularly significant, eg analytical skills in a research-based organization.

It is worth noting that the statistical approach carries a specific risk with respect to equal value. The most common statistical approach to generating weightings is through multiple regression analysis. This is used to compute a set of weighting coefficients by objective mathematical means. The analysis seeks to find the weighting combination that will most closely replicate a predetermined reference rank order of jobs. The reference ranking might be based on external market benchmarking of the test jobs or an internally derived reference ranking, such as a 'felt-fair' ranking, or by another ranking method such as paired comparison. However, unless the reference ranking has itself been developed using an objective process, the regression analysis has the potential to reinforce inequalities or preconceptions. The use of market data is particularly suspect in this respect, as pay discrimination in favour of male-dominated roles may already be embedded in the market.

Multiple regression can also lead to unhelpful statistical outcomes; for example, where a skill such as operational dexterity applies mainly to lower-level jobs, the multiple regression analysis can result in negative correlations, implying that points should be deducted for certain skills. While statistically correct, this will be a totally inappropriate and unusable outcome where a scheme is intended to address a broad range of job demands.

The use of statistical analysis therefore needs to be put in context as a starting point for weighting discussions, rather than delivering the 'right answer'. It is rare for a scheme to be able to adopt unmodified the initial weighting derived from a statistical model.

Scoring progression

Whichever approach is taken to determine overall factor weights, a further decision needs to be made on how to set the scoring progression within each factor. There are two methods. The 'arithmetic' approach assumes that there are consistent step differences between factor levels, for example a four-level factor might be scored 1, 2, 3, 4. Alternatively, geometric scoring assumes that there are progressively larger score differences at each successive level in the hierarchy. For example, the difference between the lowest two levels for an impact factor might be between impact on own work area at the lowest factor to impact on individual customers at the next factor, whereas between the highest levels the progression may be from impact on a department to impact on the whole organization. Geometric progression assumes that this distance needs to be reflected in the scoring progression. Thus the levels may be scored 1, 2, 4, 8 rather than 1, 2, 3, 4. The effect is to increase the scoring differentiation between higher-level jobs, although the impact on the overall rank order may well be small.

Another consideration is whether to apply a multiplier to all of the scores. For example, all scores may be multiplied by 10 in order to make the difference between scores look greater. This does not affect the ranking of jobs, but it can affect how the ranking is perceived; a difference of 20 points between two jobs may be perceived as more meaningful than a difference of 2 points. Having a multiplier may also be helpful at the later stage of drawing grade boundaries, when larger scores allow more line drawing opportunities.

Testing the approach

Whichever approach to scoring is adopted, it is common to try a couple or more alternative weightings and it is not unusual for the number of tests to be much higher. However, remodelling the weightings is likely to result only in marginal differences to the rank order unless significant changes are made to them. In the early 1990s, one public sector organization undertook over 50 separate analyses before agreeing their scheme weighting. One of the skills in creating the scoring model is knowing when to stop.

Finally, if a consultant has been used to develop weightings, it is important that the organization is left with a full understanding of how the ranking has been derived in order to be able to explain how the scheme is constructed. It would be the organization's and not the consultant's responsibility to explain the scheme in the event of an Employment Tribunal, should there be an equal pay claim.

Validating the rank order of roles

There is no single, simple test to confirm whether the ranking of roles generated by the scoring system is correct. After all, as stated in the EOC Good Practice Guide, job evaluation is in large part a social mechanism to establish agreed differentials within organizations.[5] Therefore, the final test is whether the resulting rank order looks reasonable to all parties, and whether the appropriate tests have been made to ensure that the scheme applies fairly to the range of jobs it will cover. This is where caution must be exercised to ensure that the rank order review does not lead to weighting adjustments aimed at reverting to the previous hierarchy of roles, based on preconceptions about their relative worth, or expectations about what results the job evaluation scheme should produce.

The validity of the rank order generated by the scoring system can be tested by comparing it with 'reference rank orders'. These are rank orders already in existence such as grades of jobs, job evaluation scores, current pay levels, external market levels, or a specially developed reference rank (the latter should have been agreed earlier in the project, typically through whole-job ranking, paired comparison, or a stacking exercise). But any tests that rely on preconceptions about the relative worth of jobs or existing job rankings must be used carefully to avoid bias.

The use of reference ranks to validate the rank order of jobs can be criticized on the grounds that the criteria are inappropriate or that the result will simply be to reproduce the status quo. The counter argument is that without anything to check against, there may be no criteria at all to assess the validity of results and validation would be an entirely subjective process. As long as reference ranks are used, perhaps in combination, as a general guide to support a robust critique of the rank order, they should support the decision-making process.

PREPARING FOR IMPLEMENTATION

Scheme design is only completed when there is a validated set of factors, a method for scoring them, an agreed process for analysing jobs, and an agreed approach and timescale for implementation. In larger organizations or for sector schemes that span a number of organizations, it may be helpful to conduct further testing or to pilot the scheme.

If a full pilot is conducted, the optimum site is one that:

▌ is self-contained;

▌ has job-evaluation-literate staff;

▌ represents as many types/levels of employees as possible;

▌ covers jobs that are sensitive from an equal value perspective;

▌ is able to engage top-level management in the communications process.

The aim of this final testing should be to use the processes that will be used in full scheme implementation. This is an opportunity to test for:

▌ how individual evaluations will flow through the process with regard to job analysis, evaluating jobs, validation of evaluations, final approval/authorization of evaluations, recording evaluation outcomes;

▌ training, roll-out and communications processes;

▌ computer support, if appropriate.

When the final testing is complete, the learning can be fed into the arrangements for full scheme implementation. This will require decisions to be made about what jobs will need to be evaluated, as well as ongoing support and appeals processes. These issues are discussed in Chapters 10 and 11.

References
1. IDS Study Plus: Autumn 2000
2. ACAS: *Job Evaluation – an Introduction*
3. E-Reward: Job evaluation survey
4. IDS Study Plus: Autumn 2000
5. Equal Opportunities Commission: *Good Practice Guide – Job Evaluation Schemes Free of Sex Bias*

8

Computer-based job evaluation

Computers have been used in job evaluation for 25 years or more and yet, according to the recent survey of job evaluation practice carried out by E-Reward,[1] 'computer-assisted job evaluation is still far from the norm'. The survey found that:

■ almost 90 per cent of respondents use a computer to calculate job evaluation scores;

■ just over half use a computer to sort and analyse job evaluation scores;

■ a similar proportion use computers to analyse completed paper questionnaires;

■ just under a quarter use the computer for the 'interactive collection of job information'.

This profile of usage reflects the chronological development of computer software for job evaluation purposes. This chapter will trace those key stages in the expansion of the use of computers in job evaluation, concluding with a comparison of two alternative approaches (including a description of Gauge, the interactive 'paperless' system referred to in Chapter 1, and the scheme provided by Link Reward Consultants).

THE TWO STAGES OF JOB EVALUATION

As explained in previous chapters, two separate and sequential aspects have to be developed for any new job evaluation system:
1) the scheme design;
2) the evaluation process.
As the first usually flows seamlessly into the second, attempting to create a clear distinction may seem artificial but, when considering the use of computers in job evaluation, this separation is important.

COMPUTERS IN SCHEME DESIGN

For the purposes of this chapter, 'scheme design' includes every step from the decision to use job evaluation in an organization through to the point at which the developed and tested factor plan is formally approved by a steering group. Any computer program/database that is to be used in the ongoing evaluation process will clearly need to be tested before it is used for the actual evaluation of any jobs, but this testing is not a part of 'scheme design' as defined above.

Factor weighting

It is in one of the key steps of scheme design – factor weighting – that the power of the computer was first used to 'improve' the quality of job evaluation. During the 1960s, computers were almost exclusively 'mainframe' installations, dedicated to the recording and administration of business data. Access was usually strictly limited and, as far as its use by the HR department for job evaluation was concerned, only applications related to the calculation and analysis of scores were normally available.

In their attempts to challenge the dominance of the Hay system of job evaluation, most of the UK consultancies majored on the importance of 'tailored' systems. They cited the benefits of unique factor plans developed specifically for the organization and, usually, by a team of people from within that organization. This, inevitably, required the determination of appropriate weightings for the chosen factors – always a contentious issue. The emerging ability of computers in the early 1970s to carry out sophisticated analyses of evaluation data and produce statistically 'correct' weightings was an opportunity not to be missed.

'Multiple linear regression analysis' (MLRA), the process of determining the relative impact of totally independent inputs on a resultant output, was the most relevant and sophisticated process available. Put in job evaluation terms, MLRA is a means to determine what factor weightings need to be applied to the basic factor scores determined for a set of test jobs in order for their total weighted scores to place them in a predetermined, 'felt fair' score order.

In the early 1970s, the complex programs involved could only be run on relatively large computers and one consultancy even had an arrangement to run its factor weighting program overnight on the Cambridge University computer – unchallengeable credentials! On first impressions, the use of MLRA to determine factor weightings has a number of key benefits, enthusiastically promoted by those consultancies using it in the 1970s (and some that still use it):

▓ It avoids all subjective or emotional debate on the relative importance of different factors.

▓ Specifically, as a process it has no element of gender bias.

▓ Weightings can be justified statistically.

▓ The 'best fit' with the predetermined score order can be demonstrated.

However, for factor weightings determined by MLRA to be 'correct', four important criteria must be met:

1. The factor plan must include every aspect of job demands that could affect the position of any job in the predetermined score order.

2. Each factor must be totally independent of every other factor (ie no 'double-counting').

3. The selection of test jobs (from which the weightings will be calculated) must be totally representative of the full job population.

4. The predetermined 'felt fair' score order of the test jobs (ie the desired output) must be totally explained by the individual factor scores and not influenced by any other variable or consideration.

As MLRA is still used today by some consultancies, it is important to explore the extent to which these conditions are likely to apply. This will allow a fair assessment of its validity as a means of determining factor weighting and the accuracy of the resulting weights.

1. The factor plan must include every aspect of job demands that could affect the position of any job in the predetermined score order

If the plan development has been carried out in the manner recommended in Chapter 7, there is every probability that this condition will have been met (but see point 4 below).

2. Each factor must be totally independent of every other factor (ie no 'double counting')

The more factors (or sub-factors) in the plan, the higher the probability that this condition will not be met. The greater the overlap (or cross-correlation) between the scores allocated to the test jobs for the two overlapping factors, the greater the distortion in the weights allocated to those factors. In effect, the factor whose scores best predict the 'felt fair' job order (ie with the best correlation) will be allocated the greater proportion of the combined weight with the balance allocated to the other factor. In extreme cases, this can lead to factor weights differing by a multiple of 5 or more or even negative weights.

(Negative weights can also result if higher scores within a factor tend to indicate a lower position in the overall 'felt fair' score order, eg working conditions, physical demands, manual dexterity, etc).

3. The selection of test jobs (from which the weightings will be calculated) must be totally representative of the full job population

If the selection of test jobs is dominated by jobs from one 'job family', MLRA will tend to produce weightings that are appropriate for that family but may not be right for the organization as a whole. For instance, if a factor has been added to the plan because it is very important for jobs in one family (and no others) but only two or three jobs scoring high on that factor are included as test jobs, the 'correlation' of that factor will be low and the MLRA process will tend to allocate it a lower weight than it merits.

4. The predetermined 'felt fair' score order of the test jobs (ie the desired output) must be totally explained by the individual factor scores and not influenced by any other variable or consideration.

This is arguably the most important criterion of all and raises the question: 'how was the target "felt-fair" score order of jobs predetermined?'

- If it is simply the existing rank order, it reflects historical attitudes about jobs (or people) and almost certainly includes an element of gender discrimination.

- If it is a 'market rate' rank order, it will be influenced by current skills shortages or surpluses, or other organizations' views on job relativities (which again could include gender bias), none of which are contained within the factor plan.

A target score order determined by a cross-section of knowledgeable people within the organization is likely to be the best option, particularly if those people were also involved in the factor analysis of the test jobs. Even here, however, there are pitfalls to be avoided.

- If the target is a rank order of the test jobs (rather than a list of scores that recognizes relative job sizes), it may not include a realistic separation of some adjacent jobs nor an appropriate 'bunching' of others. This is likely to be the case if a paired comparison process has been used to generate the rank order.

▓ If score progression in each factor is not appropriately 'arithmetic' or 'geometric' (see Chapter 2), the weightings will reflect an inappropriate scoring system.

MLRA or equivalent programs can now be run on most PCs.

Analysis of test data

Computers also provide a useful tool for the recording and detailed analysis of test data, mainly through the use of spreadsheet or database facilities. This is an essential step in testing of the scheme design and highlighting any aspects of the design that may need to be modified.

1. Individual factor levels

Sorting the list of test jobs by the levels allocated to each factor in turn will greatly assist the evaluation panel in reviewing its decisions before the design outcome is presented to the steering group, and the latter in satisfying itself that the design is sound before approving it.

As noted in Chapter 5, a useful approach is to create one printout per factor, showing the jobs listed in level order under that factor and with the total scores for the jobs (raw or weighted) also listed. The panel can then concentrate on one factor at a time, checking that they have been objective and consistent in allocating each of the levels within that factor. A high factor level for a job that has a low total score (and vice versa) may indicate an incorrect level but great care must be taken to avoid the presumption that this will always be the case.

An unusually high (or low) proportion of jobs with the same factor level may indicate a need to review the definition of that level which, in comparison with adjacent level definitions, may be too broad (or too narrow). If a level definition is changed, the panel will, of course, need to review its decisions on all jobs allocated that level or one of the adjacent levels.

2. Factor scoring and weighting

Once all the factor levels have been reviewed and amended if necessary, the provisional scoring method (arithmetic or geometric) and weighting for each factor can be reviewed. This may be seen as an additional role for the evaluation panel or project team but is more commonly viewed as a responsibility of the steering group or its equivalent.

It is relatively straightforward to set up a spreadsheet to allow the user to 'toggle' between an arithmetic progression and a geometric one for each factor in turn, with the impact of each change being shown immediately through the recalculation of the total job scores. The impact of adjusting individual factor weights up or down can also be tested in a similar manner and it is usually best to test both of these factor characteristics at the same time, as they are interdependent.

The relative impact that a factor can have on the overall rank order of jobs is determined by the combination of its 'implicit weighing' and its 'explicit weight' (see Chapter 7). As explained in that chapter, the 'implicit weight' of a factor is the ratio of the highest unweighted score available in that factor to the average highest score for all factors – this is determined by the number of levels in a factor and by the scoring progression adopted. The 'explicit weight' is the multiplier applied to all unweighted scores in that factor.

In the absence of any reason to do otherwise, it is normal practice to set the 'explicit weight' of each factor to 1.0 and to await the outcome of the testing exercise before making any decision to use any other weights. Frequently, the more important factors end up with more defined levels than the less important ones and the higher 'implicit weight' that results is all that is needed to generate the appropriate impact on the total job scores. This effect is enhanced if geometric scoring is used.

The number of levels in a factor can, however, be determined by the ease or difficulty the scheme designers had in defining clearly separate levels. This can result in an inappropriate 'implicit weighting', and applying an 'explicit weighting' is the means by which this can be redressed.

Irrespective of whether or not 'explicit weights' were identified during the design stage (eg from a 'focus group', possibly using a paired comparison approach) or after the test jobs evaluation (eg using MLRA), the steering group has the responsibility for confirming the 'explicit weightings' to be used in the finalized system. The 'what if' facility provided by a properly constructed spreadsheet or database is an essential tool in enabling them to do this.

Setting grade boundaries

As already stressed in previous chapters, determining pay is not a part of job evaluation. However, the allocation of jobs to grades (usually the immediate precursor to the development of a new pay or salary structure) can properly be seen as the final stage of job evaluation.

The various ways of developing grade structures linked to job evaluation scores are covered in Chapter 9. Alternative structures can readily be created on paper, simply by inspecting a list of evaluated jobs in score order and identifying appropriate grade boundaries. This rarely, however, provides the full picture and specifically does not calculate the cost to the organization of implementing the new structure and associated pay arrangements.

The final decision on whether or not to implement a new job evaluation system will always be influenced by the likely impact on employee costs and, if these have not been assessed, approval is unlikely to be given. The immediate cost of implementing the 'ideal' grade and salary structure will be the cost of raising the pay of those people whose current pay is less than the minimum for their new grade up to the minimum for that grade, which can be expensive.

Most of the consultancies supplying job evaluation systems or services now also provide grade or pay modelling software that will calculate implementation costs. Typically, the program will match job evaluation data and current pay for a sample of jobholders. Proposed grade boundaries and associated pay ranges can be entered separately and the combined result displayed in tabular or graphical form. The total cost of raising all jobholders to the proposed minima for their new grades will be calculated and presented – the immediate implementation cost – together with the total of the 'red circle' salary excesses for those paid more than the maximum for their new grade – the long-term recoverable cost. In a matter of minutes, various combinations of grade boundaries and pay ranges can be tested until an acceptable compromise solution is found.

The initial determination of grade boundaries is usually carried out using the results of the test job analysis but it is prudent not to finalize these until a significant proportion of all jobs have been evaluated, particularly those with multiple jobholders. The quantity of data that then has to be analysed is such that, without a relatively sophisticated computer program, effective comparison of all the options would be virtually impossible.

COMPUTERS IN THE EVALUATION PROCESS

The case for computerization

In a non-computerized paper-based scheme, jobs are usually evaluated by a panel that includes a broadly representative group of staff as well as line managers and one or more members of the HR department. The panel will have been trained in interpreting the factor plan and applying this in the evaluation of the job descriptions or questionnaires provided. The panel studies the job information and, by relating this to the factor level definitions and panel decisions on previous jobs, debates and agrees the level (and hence the score) that should be allocated for each factor. This is a well-understood process that has been tried and tested over more than 50 years and, properly applied, is generally accepted as a good approach by all concerned.

The problem with the panel approach is chiefly the way it is applied, leading to the criticisms of job evaluation outlined in Chapter 1. The most common failings or disadvantages are:

- *Inconsistent judgements*: although the initial panel is usually well trained, panel membership changes and, over time, the interpretation of the factor plan may also change. The presence or absence of a particularly strong-minded member may influence panel decisions.

- *Inadequate record of decisions*: each allocated factor level will, of necessity, be recorded but it is relatively rare for panels to maintain a complete record of how each decision was reached. If an 'appeal' is lodged, it can be difficult to assess whether or not the original panel took account of whatever evidence is presented in support of the appeal.

- *Staff input required*: the preparation and agreement of a sufficiently detailed job description will take anything from three to six person-hours. A panel of six people (a typical size) may take an hour to evaluate each job if a traditional job-by-job approach is used. Up to 10 person-hours could thus be spent evaluating each job. This is a substantial cost for any organization.

▌ *Time taken to complete process*: Assembling a quorum of trained panel members may take several weeks and, if their evaluations are subject to review by some higher-level review team (to minimize the risk of subsequent appeals), it can take two or three months to complete the whole process.

▌ *Lack of 'transparency' or involvement*: The process has a 'take it or leave it' aspect about it that is at variance with modern management practice and fosters 'appeals' resulting from ignorance of how a job score or grade was determined. The process and criteria for evaluating jobs are often unknown to most jobholders.

While, to many people, computers are inappropriate for 'people-related' activities ('impersonal', 'impenetrable', 'inflexible', etc), they have unarguable benefits that, properly used, can overcome most if not all of the failings set out above. These are:

▌ consistency;

▌ record keeping;

▌ speed;

▌ in some applications, transparency.

Consistency

This is probably the greatest benefit of any reputable computer-based job evaluation process. The same input information will always give the same output result. It is as if the original fully trained and experienced evaluation panel was permanently available and never makes a decision that conflicts with a previous decision. Of course, on initial set-up the computer might produce consistently inappropriate outputs but this will normally be corrected as part of the testing/trialling stages. The ease with which such changes can be made, for instance to update the system following a major review, is one of the aspects that differentiate some of the commercially available systems.

Record keeping

Computers now have, in effect, infinite memories and all aspects of every evaluation will be securely saved for future analysis or recall and normally 'password protected'. Even if all the relevant information is not recorded at the time of the evaluation, it can usually be added later. Most computer-based systems offer extensive database capabilities for sorting, analysing and reporting on the input information and system outputs.

Speed

The 'decision-making' process is near enough instantaneous and the elapsed time for an evaluation is thus restricted to the time taken to collect the job information and to input it to the computer. For those systems where there is no need to convene a panel, the evaluation result can be available for review as soon as the job information is complete.

Most non-computerized schemes rely on job descriptions or 'open' questionnaires that are interpreted by the evaluation panel. Computers, on the other hand, require 'closed' questionnaire responses and 'fully computerized' systems work on this approach, although most have the opportunity for free text to be added if desired to explain the choice of answer. If an organization prefers the source of job information to be 'open', then a small panel will be needed to interpret that information and input it to the system.

Transparency

The better computer-based evaluation systems enable the evaluator(s) to track the progress of an evaluation, identifying which answer(s) to which question(s) give rise to the resultant factor level – demonstrably the 'correct' level based on the factor level definitions. If jobholders subsequently challenge the result, they can be taken through the evaluation record and shown, in simple language, exactly why a different score is not justified.

Some systems, however, are no more transparent than a non-computerized approach, with the jobholder having no involvement in, nor understanding of, the steps between agreeing the job description (or questionnaire) and being told the final score or grade outcome. In some cases this 'black box' effect means that even the 'evaluators' themselves have difficulty in understanding the logic that converts the input information to a factor level score and, although the consistency will still be maintained, that may not be easy to demonstrate if challenged by a jobholder or line manager.

The authors of this book are convinced that the more recent developments in computer-based job evaluation have helped to overcome the negative image of traditional paper-based approaches, and that this has contributed significantly to the resurgence of job evaluation over the past 10 years. Improvements in objectivity, consistency, involvement, transparency, efficiency (in the use of time) and ease of administration are all potential benefits available from a good, appropriate system.

The two types of 'computer-based' job evaluation systems

The two types of system are:

1. Conventional computer-based schemes in which the job analysis data is either entered direct into the computer or transferred to it from a paper questionnaire. The computer software applies predetermined rules to convert the data into scores for each factor and produce a total score.

2. Interactive computer-based schemes in which the jobholder and his or her manager sit in front of a PC and are presented with a series of logically interrelated questions, the answers to which lead to a score for each of the built in factors in turn and a total score.

The 'conventional' type of system was the first to be made available, in the 1980s, and is still widely used. Most systems available today have been developed from their original form to take advantage of up-to-date technology, particularly Microsoft products as these are in common use and widely understood. The systems offered by different consultancies are all essentially similar, other than the way in which the 'rules' that convert the input data into scores are structured. One of the more widely used systems for general application (ie which can be used with any job evaluation scheme) is that available from Link Reward Consultants. The number of Link installations worldwide is in the hundreds and the Link system was used to deliver the Equate method designed by KPMG and its Health Sector version MedEquate. More recently, the software delivers the GLPC factor scheme developed for London Local Authorities. The Link system is outlined below.

The only genuinely 'interactive' system, Gauge, was developed in the early 1990s, once Windows technology had become widely established. It gained rapid acceptance as an alternative to the 'conventional' computerized approaches then available. As with the Link system, Gauge can also be used with any job evaluation scheme and because of the way it replicates the logic of an evaluation panel in arriving at factor scores, many of its initial applications were with clients wanting to improve the process by which their existing schemes were applied. In 1999, Gauge was selected to computerize the NJC's 'Single Status' job evaluation scheme for local authorities in England and Wales and subsequently, by COSLA, for those in Scotland. In 2002 it was adopted by the Association of Colleges to computerize the new scheme covering all jobs in Colleges of Further Education. Gauge is developed, supplied and supported by Pilat HR Solutions, and total installations worldwide also run into the hundreds.

Descriptions of the Link and Gauge systems are given below but, to avoid repetition, the common features of each (and some other leading products) are listed here:

▌ Both are software shells that can be used with any type of analytical job evaluation scheme. It would be normal for the purchaser to have a paper-based scheme already developed and tested before a computerized version was created, although, as already noted, a degree of overlap can be beneficial.

▌ For organizations that do not want to develop their own scheme from scratch, both consultancies offer a 'base' system, pre-developed and loaded on their software, that organizations can tailor to match their own circumstances.

▌ Training is provided in the evaluation process and in making the optimum use of the database capabilities (a key benefit of computerized systems).

▌ At the end of each evaluation the weighted score for the job is calculated automatically and the job placed into a rank order of evaluated positions. If grade boundaries have been pre-set, the resultant grade is also calculated.

▌ All job data is held in a database and is available for reports or further analysis. The database can be interrogated and both standard and ad hoc reports can be created.

▌ Access to the software is password protected. Each user can be assigned privileges that determine what they can do and see, and all activity is logged.

▌ Both software programs can be installed and run on a PC (desktop or notebook), the Internet and an intranet.

It should be borne in mind that it is not possible to do justice to the full 'look' and 'feel' of any software product on paper. Outline descriptions of the two main job evaluation products are given below but anyone with a serious interest in computer-based job evaluation should see the system(s) in operation, preferably with an existing user.

Link – a computer-assisted system

One of the more widely used systems for general application (ie which can be used with any job evaluation scheme) is that available from Link Reward Consultants. The number of Link installations worldwide is in the hundreds and the Link system was used to deliver the Equate method designed by KPMG and its Health Sector version MedEquate. More recently, the software delivers the GLPC factor scheme developed for London Local Authorities. The Link system is outlined below.

Basis of the process

The basis on which the Link computer-assisted system operates is the analysis of answers provided to a comprehensive range of questions about each of the scheme factors in a structured questionnaire. This questionnaire can be produced in hard copy, for completion before the data is entered into the computer, or as an on-screen questionnaire. The former typically runs to 30 or 40 pages, hence the benefits of the on-screen version.

Establishing the 'rules'

Before any data can be entered, the evaluation 'rules' have to be determined and programmed into the software. These, in effect, determine what factor level is justified by all the answers given to the questions related to the factor concerned. They are developed from analyses of completed questionnaires related to test jobs that have already been ascribed factor levels, usually by a traditional evaluation panel approach. Client staff and union representatives are often involved directly in the development of these rules.

Evaluation

Job information is gathered via an on-screen job analysis questionnaire, usually input by an analyst or evaluator. Each question has online help and the ability to review which other reference jobs have answered it – an aid to ongoing consistency. As an option the system will prompt for explanatory text to back up a response given.

The system performs a series of validation checks on the answers to different questions to identify any potential data inconsistencies. Checks are both internal (are the responses given consistent with each other?) and external to other jobs (are responses in line with other similar positions?). When all questions have been answered and all checks completed, the score for the job is calculated by the system using the inbuilt 'rules', and added to the database of completed evaluations.

Openness

As explained by Link: 'the factors and weightings are usually made known to evaluators and job analysts and often extended to all interested parties. How the evaluation rules work behind the scenes to logically produce an appropriate factor level can be relatively sophisticated and this is less likely to be disclosed for the reasons of complexity rather than secrecy.'

Feedback to jobholder

Jobholders or line managers are normally informed of the evaluation result (score or grade), after an appropriate approval process.

Gauge – the 'interactive' computer-assisted system

The Gauge software was specifically developed to promote the use of job evaluation by overcoming the principal disadvantages of traditional processes:

- time consuming, both in the overall evaluation process itself and in the elapsed time to get a job evaluated, and hence costly in management time;

- paper-intensive, in the necessary preparation of lengthy job descriptions and/or questionnaires, etc;

- open to subjective or inconsistent judgements;

- opaque in terms of how scores are determined – a criticism also levelled against 'conventional' computer-assisted systems;

- bureaucratic, and remote from jobholders themselves, inevitably leading to 'appeals' against evaluation results.

Basis of the process

The Gauge process effectively replicates the tried and tested evaluation panel approach but needs neither job descriptions nor evaluation panels. The people who know most about the job (jobholder and line manager) answer a series of logically interrelated questions on screen, supported by a trained 'facilitator'. These questions will have been pre-loaded into the system in a series of logic trees (one for each factor) and will be the questions that a skilled job evaluation panel would ask in deciding what factor score to allocate to the job being evaluated.

Building the 'question trees'

Each factor has its own set of questions, each question having a number of pre-set answers. Client staff and/or their representatives will often be directly involved in the wording of these questions and answers, developed from the panel or project team deliberations recorded during the creation of the factor plan and its checking by evaluation of the test jobs.

Evaluation

Selecting one of the answers to a question (by simply 'clicking' on it) does three things. First, it identifies and presents the most logical follow-up question; secondly, if appropriate, it progresses the scoring process; and thirdly, it contributes to the Job Overview report.

Every job is presented with the same initial question in a factor but the logic tree format means that different jobs will take different routes through the other questions in that factor. This allows progressively more relevant questions to be asked and avoids, for example, senior managers being asked questions more relevant to clerical activities and vice versa. Any one job will normally be presented with about 20 per cent of the available questions, of which there are typically 400–500 in a completed system.

The scoring process is the predetermined 'elimination' of one or more of the possible factor levels from consideration. Questioning continues until every level except one has been logically eliminated. The remaining level is recorded as the 'correct' level for that factor and the questioning moves on to the next factor. Provided that there is reasonable agreement between jobholder and manager about the job responsibilities and activities, the evaluation should take no more than one hour.

Openness

The identification of the correct factor level is a totally 'transparent' process in that the progressive elimination of the levels can be followed as each question is answered. (Even at a later time, the specific answer or sequence of answers that led to the elimination of a particular level can be demonstrated – a powerful tool in rebutting claims for higher scores.)

Feedback to jobholder

At the end of an evaluation, the system displays a 'Job Overview' which presents the information provided through the question/answer process in a narrative format. Those involved in the evaluation can read this and, if anything appears incorrect, can return to the question that gave rise to the incorrect statement and reconsider the answer. Changing an answer will usually lead to a different set of follow-up questions but will not necessarily result in a different score, even though the Job Overview will have changed. It is normal practice to allow jobholders and line managers a period of time following the evaluation to examine the Job Overview (on screen or in hard copy) before 'sign off'.

The Job Overview is thus the rationale for the score given and a score cannot be changed without answering the questions in a different way (and even this may not change the score). Anyone wishing to challenge the score for a job must show that one or more of the statements on the Job Overview is/are incorrect. It is a key document for two main reasons:

1. An 'appeal' can only be lodged on the basis that there is an incorrect statement in the Job Overview (and evidence to support this claim would be required). As the jobholder would have been a party to the acceptance of the Job Overview in the first place, the number of appeals is dramatically reduced.

2. As the Job Overview does not contain any reference to specific tasks carried out by the jobholder, hard copy of a relevant Job Overview can be shown to holders of similar jobs for them to confirm that it is equally valid for their own particular post. If so, there is no need to evaluate these posts and, furthermore, the basis for role interchangeability will have been established. Even if not, only the points of difference need to be evaluated for the new job – a substantial time saving.

Which computer-based system to use?

There is no 'one size fits all' answer to this question.

Organizations that already use a detailed paper questionnaire as part of an existing scheme would probably find the 'conventional' computerized questionnaire analysis approach quicker and cheaper to install. Those wanting to move to a 'transparent' system that involves jobholders in the evaluation of their own jobs will probably find the 'interactive' approach preferable.

As in all such situations, it is the process that 'fits' best with the organization's other HR processes that is most likely to be accepted by all interested parties. This can only be judged by looking carefully at each approach and, preferably, having at least two alternative systems demonstrated to an appropriate selection panel.

Reference
1.   E-Reward.co.uk: Research Report no. 7, January 2003

9

Grade and pay structure design

The outcome of a job evaluation exercise is usually a new or revised grade and pay structure. The purpose of this chapter is to describe how job evaluation can be used to initiate or contribute to the design process for the various types of grade and pay structures that are available. The chapter starts with definitions of grade and pay structures and continues with an assessment of the considerations affecting their design. It then describes how job evaluation is used in the design process – generally and for particular structures. Equal value considerations are dealt with at the end of the chapter.

GRADE AND PAY STRUCTURES

At the outset, a distinction needs to be made between grade and pay structures: *grade structures* contain a sequence or hierarchy of grades, bands or levels into which, on the basis of job evaluation, groups of jobs which are broadly comparable in size are placed; *pay structures* define the ranges of pay that are attached to grades – pay levels will be influenced by equity and market rate considerations.

Grade structures

In grade structures, jobs are initially allocated into grades, bands or levels following a job evaluation exercise. The subsequent maintenance of the grade structure by grading or regrading jobs is also carried out with the help of analytical job evaluation or, sometimes, by a process of 'matching' the role profiles of jobs under review with grade definitions.

There may be a single structure with a sequence of narrow grades (often between nine and twelve), or there may be a broad-banded structure with relatively few much wider bands (often four to five). In between these two there might be what is sometimes called a 'fat grade' structure with between six and eight grades. Alternatively, the structure may consist of a number of career or job families which group jobs with similar characteristics in terms of activities and knowledge and skill requirements together. Each family is typically divided into six to eight levels. Career family structures define career paths in each family and have common grades and pay ranges across all families. Job family structures also define career paths but the families have different grades and pay ranges.

The grades, bands or levels may be defined in one or other of the following ways or a combination of them:

- by means of a range of job evaluation points – jobs are allocated to a grade, band or level if their job evaluation scores fall within a range or bracket of points;

- in words which describe the characteristics of the work carried out in the jobs that are positioned in each grade or level – these grade, band or level definitions may set out the key activities and the competences or knowledge and skills required at different points in the hierarchy;

- by reference to benchmark jobs or roles that have already been placed in the grade, band or job family level.

Pay structures

Pay structures provide a framework for managing pay. They contain the organization's pay ranges or scales for jobs grouped into grades, bands or job family levels. These define the different levels of pay for jobs or groups of jobs by reference to their relative internal value as determined by job evaluation, to external relativities as established by market rate surveys and, where appropriate, to negotiated rates for jobs. They provide scope for pay progression in accordance with performance, competence, contribution or service.

A grade structure becomes a pay structure when pay ranges or brackets are defined for each grade, band or level, or when grades are attached to a pay spine. For example, a '40 per cent' pay range linked to a grade could span from £20,000 to £28,000. Pay ranges are often described as a percentage of the mid-point; for example, the range could be expressed as 80 to120 per cent where the mid-point is £25,000 and the minimum and maximum are £20,000 and £30,000 respectively. The mid-point, often referred to as the reference point or target salary, may be regarded as the rate for a fully competent individual and is usually aligned to market rates in accordance with company policies on the relationship between its pay levels and market rates for similar jobs (this is sometimes called the 'market stance').

The main varieties of pay structures follow the pattern of grade structures referred to above:

▍ narrow graded structures with fairly small pay ranges attached to them;

▍ 'fat graded' structures with fewer grades and wider pay ranges;

▍ broad-banded structures with a limited number of broad bands within each of which the range of pay may be much greater than in either of the above two structures – reference points and pay zones may be placed within the bands and these define the rates and range of pay for the individual jobs or clusters of jobs allocated to each band;

▨ career or job family structures within which each family will have levels to which pay ranges are attached.

In addition, pay spines are found in the public and not-for-profit sectors which consist of a series of pay points to which are attached grades.

There may be a single pay structure covering the whole organization or there may be more than one structure for staff and another for manual workers. Senior executives are sometimes treated separately. Pay structures may incorporate spot rates or individual job grades as described below.

Spot rates

'Spot rates' are rates of pay for jobs or people which are not located within grades and for which there is no defined scope for pay progression. They may be used for some jobs such as those at senior management levels which the organization wants to keep separate from the grade structure, usually in order to have more scope to pay what they want. Some organizations do not have a graded structure at all and only use spot rates. Spot rates may be attached to a person rather than a job. Jobholders may be eligible for incentive bonuses on top of the spot rate but consolidated increases in pay related to performance simply result in a new spot rate for the person. Relativities between spot rates can be determined by job evaluation, but the key factor is often market relativities for the job or the market worth of the person.

Spot rates are frequently used by organizations that want the maximum amount of scope to vary the pay for individuals or jobs. They are often adopted by small or start-up organizations which do not want to be constrained by a formal grade structure and prefer to retain the maximum amount of flexibility. Spot rates are also the traditional basis for manual jobs. The focus of this chapter, however, is on graded pay structures because they provide a better basis for managing grading and pay consistently within a defined framework and, as such, are the most typical approach.

Individual job grades

Individual job grades are, in effect, spot rates to which a defined pay range of, say, 10 to 15 per cent on either side of the rate has been attached to provide scope for pay progression based on performance, competence or contribution. Again, the mid-point of the range is fixed by reference to job evaluation and market rate comparisons.

Individual grades are attached to jobs, not persons, but there may be more flexibility for movement between grades than in a conventional grade structure when, for example, a person has expanded his or her role and it is considered that this growth in the level of responsibility needs to be recognized without having to upgrade the job. Individual job grades may be restricted to certain jobs, for example more senior managers where flexibility in fixing and increasing rates of pay is felt to be desirable.

The 'zones' that are often established in broad-banded structures have some of the characteristics of individual job grades.

RATIONALE FOR GRADE AND PAY STRUCTURES

Grade and pay structures are needed to provide a logically designed framework within which an organization's pay policies can be implemented. They enable the organization to determine where jobs should be placed in a hierarchy, define pay levels and the scope for pay progression and provide the basis upon which relativities can be managed, equal pay achieved and the processes of monitoring and controlling the implementation of pay practices can take place. A grade and pay structure is also a medium through which the organization can communicate the career and pay opportunities available to employees.

CRITERIA FOR GRADE AND PAY STRUCTURES

Grade and pay structures should:

▌ be appropriate to the culture, characteristics and needs of the organization and its employees;

▌ ideally be internally equitable and externally competitive, although in practice this may be difficult to achieve when external market pressures mean that objectively justified higher market rates have to be paid which override internal equity considerations;

▌ facilitate the management of relativities and the achievement of fairness, consistency and transparency in managing gradings and pay;

▌ facilitate operational flexibility and continuous development;

▌ provide scope as required for rewarding performance, contribution and increases in skill and competence;

▌ clarify reward, lateral development and career opportunities;

▌ be constructed logically and clearly so that the basis upon which they operate can readily be communicated to employees;

▌ enable the organization to exercise control over the implementation of pay policies and budgets.

GRADE STRUCTURE DESIGN CONSIDERATIONS

Following a job evaluation exercise, the first consideration is the basis upon which its outcomes will be used to inform the design process. This is dealt with in the next section of this chapter. The other main points to consider are the number of grades and their width.

Number of grades

The considerations to be taken into account when deciding on the number of grades are:

▌ decisions on where grade boundaries should be placed following a job evaluation exercise which has produced a ranked order of jobs – this might identify the existence of clearly defined clusters of jobs at the various levels in the hierarchy between which there are significant differences in job size;

▨ the range and types of roles to be covered by the structure;

▨ the range of pay and points scores to be accommodated;

▨ the number of levels in the organizational hierarchy;

▨ the fact that within a given range of pay and responsibility, the greater the number of grades the smaller their width, and vice versa – this is associated with views on what is regarded as the desirable width of a range, taking into account the scope for progression, the size of increments in a pay spine and equal pay issues;

▨ the problem of 'grade drift' (unjustified upgradings in response to pressure or because job evaluation has been applied laxly) which can be increased if there are too many narrow grades.

Typically, conventional graded structures tend to have between eight and twelve grades. The structure recently developed for the NHS has eight common pay bands (the top one divided into four ranges) placed upon two pay spines, one for staff covered by the review body for nurses and other health professionals, the other for non-review-body staff. Each pay band has a corresponding range of job evaluation scores derived from the national job evaluation scheme. There is a third pay spine for doctors and dentists.

Width of grades

The factors affecting decisions on the width of grades are:

▨ views on the scope that should be allowed for progression;

▨ equal pay considerations – wide grades, especially extended incremental scales, are a major cause of pay gaps between men and women simply because women, who are more likely to have career breaks than men, may not have the same opportunity as men to progress to the upper regions of the range; male jobs may therefore cluster towards the top of the range while women's jobs may cluster towards the bottom;

▓ decisions on the number of grades – the greater the number the smaller the width;

▓ decisions on the value of increments in a pay spine – if it is believed that the number of increments should be restricted, for equal pay or other reasons, but that the number of grades should also be limited, then it is necessary to increase the value of the increments.

THE USE OF JOB EVALUATION IN DEVELOPING A GRADE STRUCTURE AND GRADING JOBS

There are three ways in which job evaluation can be used generally to develop a grade structure and grade jobs: 1) by dividing the rank order produced by an analytical job evaluation exercise into grades or bands, 2) by validating a 'matching' process following the design of a career or job family structure, or 3) through the use of a non-analytical job classification scheme which might, however, be validated by the use of an analytical job evaluation scheme.

Grading in a narrow-graded structure following an analytical job evaluation exercise

An analytical job evaluation exercise will produce a rank order of jobs according to their job evaluation scores. A decision then has to be made on where the boundaries which will define grades should be placed in the rank order. So far as possible, boundaries should divide groups or clusters of jobs which are significantly different in size so that all the jobs placed in a grade are clearly smaller than the jobs in the next higher grade and larger than the jobs placed in the next lower grade.

Fixing grade boundaries is one of the most critical aspects of grade structure design following an analytical job evaluation exercise. It requires judgement – the process is not scientific and it is rare to find a situation when there is one right and obvious answer. In theory, grade boundaries could be determined by deciding on the number of grades in advance and then dividing the rank order into equal parts. But this would mean drawing grade boundary lines arbitrarily and the result could be the separation of groups of jobs which should properly be placed in the same grade.

The best approach is to analyse the rank order to identify any significant gaps in the points scores between adjacent jobs. These natural breaks in points scores will then constitute the boundaries between clusters of jobs which can be allocated to adjacent grades. A distinct gap between the highest-rated job in one grade and the lowest-rated job in the grade above will help to justify the allocation of jobs between grades. It will therefore reduce boundary problems leading to dissatisfaction with gradings when the distinction is less well defined. Provisionally, it may be decided in advance, when designing a conventional graded structure, that a certain number of grades is required but the gap analysis will confirm the number of grades that is appropriate, taking into account the natural divisions between jobs in the rank order. However, the existence of a number of natural breaks cannot be guaranteed, which means that judgement has to be exercised as to where boundaries should be drawn when the scores between adjacent jobs are close.

In cases where there are no obvious natural breaks the guidelines that should be considered when deciding on boundaries are as follows:

▌ Jobs with common features as indicated by the job evaluation factors are grouped together so that a distinction can be made between the characteristics of the jobs in different grades – it should be possible to demonstrate that the jobs grouped into one grade resemble each other more than they resemble jobs placed in adjacent grades.

▌ The grade hierarchy should take account of the organizational hierarchy, ie jobs in which the job holder reports to a higher level job holder should be placed in a lower grade, although this principle should not be followed slavishly when an organization is over-hierarchical with, perhaps, a series of one-over-one reporting relationships.

▓ The boundaries should not be placed between jobs mainly carried out by men and jobs mainly carried out by women.

▓ The boundaries should ideally not be placed immediately above jobs in which large numbers of people are employed.

▓ The grade width in terms of job evaluation points should represent a significant step in demand as indicated by the job evaluation scheme.

The same approach can be used when designing broad-banded or fat grade structures, although it is more likely that the number of bands or grades will have been determined beforehand. The aim will still be to achieve clear distinctions between the jobs clustered in successive bands. This may be easier because there will be fewer boundary lines to draw, but unless they can be defined by reference to significant gaps the decision may still be judgemental.

The role of job evaluation in the design of career or job family structures

The design of a career family structure can be based on job evaluation by the grading process described above following the use of an analytical job evaluation scheme to produce a rank order of jobs. Alternatively, analytical job evaluation can be used in the design of either career or job families to validate prior decisions on grades and levels and the allocation of jobs to levels by matching role profiles to level definitions. In both approaches it is necessary to decide on the families required (usually not more than three or four) and how they should be defined.

When the design of a career family structure follows an analytical job evaluation exercise, the grades or levels determined by reference to the rank order produced by job evaluation are in effect sliced up into families. Career ladders are devised by defining the levels for each family in terms of the key activities carried out and the skills and knowledge (competences) required. Each level is also defined by reference to a range of job evaluation points. Benchmark jobs are allocated to levels according to their points scores but, once the design has been confirmed, many organizations allocate jobs to levels simply by matching role profiles with level definitions, although job evaluation scores can always be consulted to validate the allocation and to check that equal value considerations have been met.

When the design of a career or job family structure is based on *a priori* decisions on the number and definition of levels without reference to job evaluation scores, the first step is to select benchmark roles, which may be generic, and prepare role profiles defining the key activities carried out and the knowledge and skills required. The role profiles are then 'matched' with the level definitions in order to determine the allocation of the roles to levels. The role profiles may readily match one level but they often fit parts of one level definition and parts of another. In this case judgement is required to achieve the best general fit. It should be noted that unless 'matching' is done on an analytical basis, ie against a defined set of factors, it may lead to pay discrimination and would not provide a defence in an equal pay claim.

For this reason, although analytical job evaluation is not always used by organizations which have introduced career or job family structures, it is generally accepted that it provides necessary support to the design process and rigour from an equal value perspective. An analytical job evaluation scheme will validate the level allocations, define the levels in points terms and ensure that equal pay considerations are met within and across career families. The allocation of benchmark or generic roles to levels is recorded so that at later stages role profiles prepared for the job to be graded can be matched with benchmark role profiles as well as with the level definition.

Grade structure design based upon job classification

The non-analytical job classification method of job evaluation, as described in Chapter 2, starts with a definition of the number and characteristics of the grades into which jobs will be placed. These *a priori* decisions are made without reference to job evaluation scores, as is sometimes the case when designing career or job family structures.

There are therefore no problems in defining grade boundaries, as can occur when the structure is derived from the rank order produced by an analytical evaluation exercise.

When the grade definitions have been produced, jobs are slotted into the grades. This should ideally be carried out by means of a matching process which is analytical to the degree that it specifically compares the characteristics of whole jobs with the characteristics set out in the grade definitions.

Job classification is the simplest method of grade design but, when there is no analytical base, grading decisions may be arbitrary and inequitable. Most importantly, no reliable defence will be available in the event of an equal pay claim. The solution to these problems adopted by some organizations is to use an analytical points-factor scheme to validate the gradings and check on internal equity.

DEVELOPING PAY STRUCTURES

The pay structures for all the structures referred to above, except broad-banded structures, are devised by attaching pay ranges to each grade or level. Broad-banded structures may or may not have bands with defined pay ranges but in either case they may include pay zones for jobs or clusters of jobs within a band.

In structures other than broad-banded structures, all jobs placed in a particular grade will be paid within the range for that grade and will progress through the range on the basis of service, performance, competence or contribution. Progression within a range may be limited by thresholds which can only be crossed if defined levels of performance and competence have been achieved. The pay ranges are determined by reference to the existing rates of pay for the jobs allocated to each grade and their market rates. An analysis of market rates forms part of the pay structure design programme but in practice it may not always be possible to get reliable information for all the jobs, especially those for which good external matches are difficult to make.

Designing pay structures other than broad-banded structures

The following steps are required:

1. List the jobs placed within each grade on the basis of job evaluation (these might be limited to benchmark jobs that have been evaluated but there must be an adequate number of them if a proper basis for the design is to be provided).

2. Establish the actual rates of pay of the jobholders.

3. For each grade set out the range of pay for jobholders and calculate their average or median rate of pay (the pay practice point). It is helpful to plot this pay practice data as illustrated in Figure 9.1, which shows pay in each grade against job evaluation scores and includes a pay practice trend line.

4. Obtain information on the market rates for benchmark jobs where available. If possible, this should indicate the median rate and the upper and lower quartiles.

5. Agree policy on how the organization's pay levels should relate to market rates – its 'market stance'. This could be at the median, or above the median if it is believed that pay levels should be more competitive.

6. Calculate the average market rates for the benchmark jobs in each grade according to pay stance policy, eg the median rates. This produces the range market reference point.

7. Compare the practice and market reference points in each range and decide on the range reference point. This usually becomes the mid-point of the pay range for the grade and is regarded as the competitive rate for a fully competent jobholder in that grade. This is a judgemental process which takes into account the difference between the practice and policy points, the perceived need to be more competitive if policy rates are higher, and the likely costs of increasing rates.

8. Examine the pay differentials between reference points in adjacent grades. These should provide scope to recognize increases in job size and, so far as possible, variations between differentials should be kept to a minimum. If differentials are too close – less than 10 per cent – many jobs become borderline cases which can result in a proliferation of appeals and arguments about grading. Large differentials below senior management level of more than 25 per cent can create problems for marginal or borderline cases because of the amount at stake. Experience has shown that in most organizations with conventional grade structures, a differential of between 15 and 20 per cent is appropriate except, perhaps, at the highest levels.

9. Decide on the range of pay around the reference point. The most typical arrangement is to allow 20 per cent on either side, thus if the reference point is 100 per cent, the range is from 80 per cent to 120 per cent. The range can, however, vary in accordance with policy on the scope for progression and, if a given range of pay has to be covered by the structure, the fewer the grades the wider the ranges.

10. Decide on the extent, if any, to which pay ranges should overlap. Overlap recognizes that an experienced jobholder at the top of a range may be making a greater contribution than an inexperienced jobholder at the lower end of the range above. Large overlaps of more than 10 per cent can create equal pay problems where, as is quite common, men are clustered at the top of their grades and women are more likely to be found at the lower end.

11. Review the impact of the above pay range decisions on the pay of existing staff. Establish the number of staff whose present rate of pay is above or below the pay range for the grade into which their jobs have been placed and the extent of the difference between the rate of pay of those below the minimum and the lowest point of that pay range. Calculate the costs of bringing them up to the minimum. Software such as the pay modellers produced by Link and Pilat can be used for this purpose.

12. When the above steps have been completed, it may be necessary to review the decisions made on the grade structure and pay reference points and ranges. Iteration is almost always necessary to obtain a satisfactory result which conforms to the criteria for grade and pay structures mentioned earlier and minimizes the cost of implementation. Alternatives can be modelled using the software mentioned above.

Broad-banded pay structures

The definition of bands and the allocation of jobs into bands in a broad-banded structure may be based on job evaluation, as described earlier in this chapter. The most common approach to the definition of pay levels within bands is to insert reference points

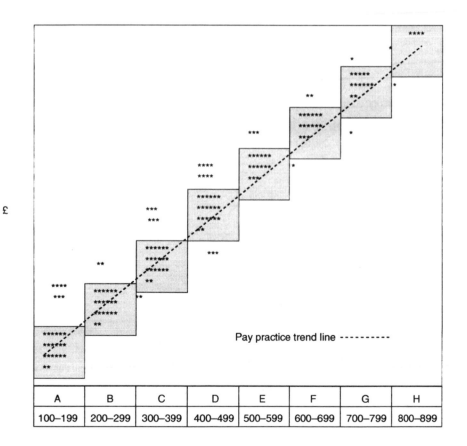

£

A	B	C	D	E	F	G	H
100–199	200–299	300–399	400–499	500–599	600–699	700–799	800–899

Pay practice trend line ----------

Figure 9.1 Scattergram of evaluations and pay

indicating the rates for individual jobs or clusters of jobs. These reference points are aligned to market rates and may be surrounded by pay ranges to form a zone. If an organization is 'market driven', that is, it attaches importance to market rate relativities, broad-banding is said to allow for greater flexibility in responding to market rate pressures than more conventional structures. It is also claimed by supporters of broad-banding that it provides for role flexibility. In a zoned band, movement to a higher zone can take place when it is evident that the role an individual is carrying out matches the role carried out by people in the higher zone. It is not dependent on the evaluation score of their job, and re-evaluations are not required unless matching is difficult or there are equal pay considerations. Zones of the type described above are not usually defined as a hierarchy within a band. In some broad-banded structures, there is scope for creating a special zone for individuals whose role has enlarged significantly but not enough to justify allocation to a higher zone in the band.

This feature of broad-banded structures means that their design is mainly dependent on decisions concerning reference points and zones (the range of the latter is often smaller than the typical range in a conventional structure, typically 10 per cent on either side of the reference point). The flexibility resulting from their use and the fact that overall, the span of pay covered by a broad band is much wider, means that few anomalies are created and the cost of implementation will therefore be much lower. This is an argument for broad-banding which is seldom revealed in public.

The various types of flexibility that broad-banding provides have made it an attractive proposition to many organizations. Generally, however, it has been found that broad-banded structures are harder to manage than narrower graded structures in spite of the original claim that they would be easier – they make considerable demands on line managers as well as HR. Broad-banding can build employee expectations of significant pay opportunities which are doomed in many cases if proper control of the system is maintained. It can be difficult to explain to people how broad-banding works and how they will be affected, and decisions on movements within bands can be harder to justify objectively than in other types of grade and pay structures. Employees may be concerned by the apparent lack of structure and precision. Above all, they create formidable equal pay problems as described in the next section of this chapter.

EQUAL VALUE CONSIDERATIONS

General considerations

The design process should minimize the risk of discrimination for any of the following reasons:

▌ The grade boundary lines in a multi-graded structure are based purely on judgements which may simply reinforce existing inequities.

▌ Generic role profiles take insufficient account of significant differences between male and female roles.

▌ An analytical job evaluation scheme is not used to define grades or allocate jobs to grades – whole jobs are slotted into a graded, broad-banded or career/job family structure by a process of internal benchmarking which could simply perpetuate existing discrimination.

▌ Benchmark jobs do not fairly represent the distribution of male and female jobs.

▌ Market-related pay levels and differentials reproduce marketplace gender discrimination and do not take account of internal relativities.

Considerations applying to particular structures

The purest type of pay structure from an equal value perspective is a spot rate structure based on one non-discriminatory job evaluation scheme with spot rate salaries relating to job evaluation points scores, which have also been checked for their discriminatory impact. However, spot rate structures supported by analytical job evaluation are rare in practice.

Narrow graded structure

The next cleanest type of system is a narrow graded structure based on a non-discriminatory job evaluation scheme, where the reference point or mid-point salary relates to the job evaluation points range, but there is a 'learning' zone below the reference point through which individuals progress as they demonstrate competence. Above the reference point individuals can receive further increases for exceptional achievement.

The main advantage of this type of structure from an equal value perspective is that it is transparent and easy to ensure that there is equal pay for female- and male-dominated groups whose jobs have been rated as equivalent under the single job evaluation scheme.

The length of the scales in an incremental system is significant. It is generally agreed (and European Court of Justice decisions support this belief) that short incremental progression scales can be justified by reference to competence or contribution. Longer incremental scales are more difficult to justify.

Discrete job evaluation points ranges imply discrete pay ranges. Overlapping scales are commonly justified by saying that an employee with a less demanding job but considerable experience is of equal worth to the organization as an employee in a more demanding job, but with less experience. This type of justification becomes more difficult to make out the greater the degree of overlap. There is risk of equal pay claims where higher graded but less experienced women are paid less than lower graded but more experienced men.

Broad-banded structures

Broad-banded structures are the most likely to lead to pay discrimination for the following reasons:

▌ Women are assimilated or started in the band in the lower part of the pay range, while men are more likely to have been assimilated towards the top because of their previous experience, grade or level of pay – women may then find it impossible or at least difficult to catch up with their male colleagues.

▌ Reliance on external relativities to place jobs in bands can reproduce existing discriminatory practices in the marketplace.

▌ The broader pay ranges within bands mean that they include jobs of widely different values or sizes which may result in gender discrimination.

▌ Insufficient attention may have been given to relative job size when placing jobs in bands because priority has been given to market rate considerations.

▌ Non-analytical whole-job comparisons have been used to slot jobs into bands or jobholders into higher zones in bands.

Career family structure

In some ways this is simply a different way of presenting a single grade structure. However, there may be problems in relation to jobs that do not easily fit into any of the agreed career families, especially if they are occupied by women and are disadvantaged in pay terms, for example if confined to an inappropriate job family. The other points made for single graded structures also apply to this type of structure.

Job family structure with variable grades

This type of structure is superficially attractive because it allows what looks like tailored grade and pay practice for each job family. It may also suggest a less radical, and therefore a less expensive, change from current systems. However, there are three potential difficulties. First, the different job evaluation grade ranges for different job families could lead to 'work rated as equivalent' equal pay claims. Second, a common justification for variations in pay for 'work rated as equivalent' jobs in different job families is market forces, but these do not always apply, or at least not to the same degree, to a whole job family (eg higher than average pay is almost certainly justified for IT specialists such as Web site designers and Oracle programmers but may not be for standard systems analysts). And third, where a female-dominated job family has a lower range of pay than a male-dominated job family, this may be subject to equal pay challenge. The points made above about length of scales and overlapping scales apply to this model also.

CONCLUSION

As described in this chapter, there are a number of ways in which analytical job evaluation can be used to ensure that robust grade structures are developed. It is up to the organization to weigh up and address the equal pay challenges presented by different types of structure, whether in the initial design or by rigorous monitoring of how it is used.

10

Introducing job evaluation

This chapter addresses the decisions and activities that are normally involved in applying job evaluation throughout an organization, either to all jobs or to the pre-defined range the system is intended to cover. It assumes that an appropriate scheme has already been selected (a proprietary scheme) or developed (a tailored scheme), thoroughly tested as described in Chapter 7 and approved or accepted by senior management and staff representatives (if relevant). The following topics are covered:

▌ development of an implementation plan;

▌ communication;

▌ operating manual;

▌ training;

▌ scheduling the evaluation programme;

▌ evaluating jobs;

- review/audit/moderation of results;

- disclosure of results;

- evaluation reviews;

- finalizing pay ranges;

- pay assimilation and protection;

- ensuring equal value.

IMPLEMENTATION PLAN

Organizations rarely need much persuasion on the need for a well-thought-out project plan for the development of a new job evaluation scheme (Chapter 7). Sadly, however, they are less likely to create an equally rigorous plan for the implementation phase, although there is a strong argument that this is even more important.

Scheme development and testing involves only a relatively small number of people and the remainder of the staff may well regard this process as an HR project with no immediate impact on themselves. Project over-run may (and should) cause embarrassment to the HR function but seldom causes major upset elsewhere – 'getting it right' is more important than delivery by a pre-set date.

Once implementation starts, however, all staff will be involved in some way or other and they will know that their pay may be affected by the outcomes. From a morale and credibility aspect, it is essential that a well-constructed timetable for implementation is developed and communicated before 'live evaluations' begin, and then adhered to. Expectations, positive or negative, will exist and timing will be one of these – late delivery will not readily be forgiven.

Initiating the plan

It is never too soon to start drafting the implementation plan. Ideally, this plan should be presented to the steering group as part of the final presentation of the development project so that approval of the scheme design and the 'go ahead' for its introduction can be given at the same time. Doing this has a number of advantages:

▌ It will pre-empt the questions about implementation that would otherwise inevitably arise.

▌ The transition from development to implementation can be portrayed as 'seamless'.

▌ The ongoing role of the steering group can be emphasized or the transfer of responsibility to another, equally authoritative, body can be effected.

▌ The full support of 'senior management' for the implementation plan can be sought and obtained.

This last point is particularly important. Implementation is a major logistical exercise and its timely progress and completion will depend on everyone adhering to commitments on the delivery of information and attendance at meetings. This will only happen if it is made clear from the outset that the implementation of job evaluation is a high priority for the organization and that dates agreed must be met.

The implementation plan should cover each of the sections that follow.

COMMUNICATION

The communication required for effective implementation of job evaluation falls into three, or sometimes four, distinct categories:

▌ briefing for managers;

▌ briefing for staff representatives (where these exist);

▌ general communication to all staff;

▌ communication to individuals prior to the analysis or evaluation of their own job.

Managers

In addition to the general communication set out below, managers should be briefed on their specific responsibilities within the overall process:

▐ the need for scrupulous objectivity and accuracy in the provision of information to the process, separating job content from jobholder qualities;

▐ the need to allow staff members time to participate in the process and to insist that appointments, once made, are kept;

▐ their own role in managing staff expectations, answering queries and, where appropriate, approving job gradings before these are made known to their own staff.

A good approach to this is to use a cascade approach down the managerial structure, with each briefing meeting covering one peer group and being chaired by a more senior manager. A job evaluation specialist should be present to explain the practical details but the senior manager should declare the organization's support of, and commitment to, the implementation programme, with particular reference to maintaining timescales.

Staff representatives

Where an organization is developing a new scheme as a joint exercise, some staff representatives will have played a full part in the scheme design and testing. It will be important to make sure that these representatives, plus any others who were not directly involved, understand the changed role that they have during implementation, for example:

▐ While any staff member should have the right to have his/her representative in attendance during any information collection process, the representative may only comment on the ways in which the process is conducted or the jobholder is treated; he/she may not challenge nor interfere with the actual information being provided.

▌ Staff representatives who are members of the evaluation panel or equivalent must put aside any allegiances to specific staff groups while carrying out their duties as evaluators.

General

Regular and pertinent communication with staff is just as important throughout the implementation programme as it is during the scheme development and many of the same aspects need to be covered.

1. Managing expectations

▌ Restate the intention behind bringing in the new job evaluation scheme.

▌ Explain again that job evaluation is not linked to measuring individual performance.

▌ Make it clear that no specific pay decisions will be made until the evaluation programme is complete (if that is the case).

▌ Reconfirm that no-one's pay will be reduced as a result of introducing the scheme.

▌ Stress that, for most people, pay will not increase.

2. Evaluation programme

▌ Explain in brief the evaluation process, who is involved and what their different roles are.

▌ Present the outline programme; if this is likely to last longer than people expect, stress the time required to do a thorough job.

▌ Present the principles of the new grade structure and, if appropriate, the new pay arrangements before any individual grades are made known.

▌ Set a timetable for communication activity.

▌ Provide regular reports on progress.

Continue the communication methods used during the development, focusing on those that proved most effective. Ideas from Chapter 7 are:

▌ Provide a telephone help line number, using an answerphone to collect questions.

▌ Give out contact numbers and e-mail addresses of all key participants.

▌ Create distinctive communications; for example, special bulletins on coloured paper.

▌ Put information on the intranet and update this regularly.

▌ Brief staff regularly through team meetings, directors' meetings and any other regular communications briefings.

▌ In particular, run full briefing meetings for staff immediately before jobs in their part of the organization are to be evaluated (the grapevine from those already evaluated will almost certainly have provided distorted information).

▌ Use a range of media, to take account of the fact that different people receive and absorb communications messages in different ways (visual, auditory, written).

Individual

Immediately prior to their personal involvement in the evaluation process, members of staff should be given a brief note explaining what they will be required to do and, if appropriate, providing information about the scheme itself. The nature of this note will vary according to the evaluation process used; an example is provided in Appendix 8 of the briefing note provided by an organization that uses the Gauge system.

OPERATING MANUAL

In Chapter 1, job evaluation was defined as 'a systematic process… to establish internal relativities…'. The only way this will be achieved is for the evaluation process to be very carefully thought out and then specified in an operating manual that becomes the authoritative document for all questions related to the development and application of job evaluation in the organization. Drafting of this manual should start during the development phase and be completed before the implementation programme starts.

The full operating manual will contain a number of sections or appendices and it may be appropriate to produce sub-manuals that contain only one or two sections, selected for specific readerships. A typical full manual would include sections covering most of the following:

- purpose of job evaluation within the organization;

- description of the scheme development, including testing (the full factor plan, scoring method and test results would normally be included as appendices);

- how job information is collected;

- how jobs are evaluated;

- how results are audited or moderated;

- how the principles of equal value should be observed in all the above steps;

- how jobholders are informed of the result and what detail is provided;

- how requests for reviews of gradings should be made and will be dealt with;

- how the system will be maintained in the longer term.

The final version of the operating manual should be approved by the steering group and any subsequent changes should first be approved by that group.

TRAINING

It almost goes without saying that all those involved in the evaluation of jobs need to be thoroughly trained in the overall system, their specific roles within the evaluation process itself and equal value requirements. As with all HR processes, consistency of application is all-important and the training should be primarily directed at achieving this objective. Specific training courses (which will vary according to the evaluation process adopted) should be developed for each of the following roles:

- interviewers/analysts who collect job information in a format for others to use;

- analysts or evaluation panel members who evaluate jobs using paper-based systems;

- analysts or facilitators who support evaluations using computerized systems;

- review or moderation panel members who examine initial evaluation results and requests for reviews and approve final results;

- review panel members who deal with requests for grading reviews immediately after the results have been announced or at a later date.

Training in the avoidance of bias (gender or other) should be an element of each of the above courses, specific to the activities involved. This should minimize the risk of discrimination in the implementation of job evaluation and also demonstrate to others that all appropriate efforts are being made to avoid bias.

Full training should be provided before any of the people above are first involved with 'live' evaluations, but this is not a one-off activity. Refresher training should take place on a regular basis to ensure that the original principles and standards are adhered to.

When new people are brought in to fulfil one of the roles, as will inevitably happen, they need to be given the full initial training first. Ideally, they should also attend one of the refresher training sessions with 'seasoned' practitioners before first taking up their role, so that they can absorb any 'custom and practice' that has evolved and thus ensure that consistency is maintained.

SCHEDULING THE EVALUATION PROGRAMME

Separate scheduling has to be done at the macro and the micro levels – the former to establish the overall programme timing (as part of the implementation plan) and the latter to ensure that specific information gathering and evaluations take place when required.

The overall programme

The first thing to establish is whether there is a pre-set date by which the whole programme has to be completed (for organizational or other outside reasons) or, if not, what the longest acceptable period would be. Once the decision to implement has been taken, most 'stakeholders' will want completion as soon as is practicable, although if, for example, the implementation cost is going to be high, management may well be happy for the full implementation to be delayed as much as possible.

In any large programme it will be very important to keep up the momentum, particularly if the existing pay/grading system is suspect. Job evaluation has in the past, with some justification, been seen as a never-ending exercise and this should be avoided at all cost. If it is going to take a year or more to cover all the jobs in the organization, the programme should be broken down into phases of not more than three or four months so that genuine progress can be demonstrated and announced at regular intervals.

What jobs?

The decision on whether jobs throughout the organization are to be evaluated using the new scheme, or only those in defined employee groups, should have been taken at the start of the design phase (see Chapter 7) but it is worth reconfirming this before creating the implementation plan. It may be that, as a result of the development and testing process, the initial decision should or has to be reviewed.

If the new scheme is primarily intended to provide more objectivity in allocating jobs to an existing grade structure, one approach would be to give priority to those jobs that have been submitted for regrading plus new jobs as yet ungraded. An extension of this is also to evaluate, as a matter of routine, any job where there is to be a change of jobholder. It would not be appropriate to make these the only criteria for selecting jobs for evaluation under the new scheme, tempting though that might be. It would take a long time for jobs that are currently over-graded to be brought in line – a potential source of equal value claims. A full programme covering all jobs should also be implemented.

Another key decision is whether every person will have their job evaluated separately, whether every discrete job with multiple jobholders will be evaluated, whether only 'generic' jobs typifying a job type will be evaluated or whether the majority of jobs will be 'slotted' into grades after a range of 'benchmarks' have been established. Clearly, moving from the first to the last of those options substantially reduces the number of evaluations required, although it should be noted that the last option may not conform to the requirements of equal pay law (see Chapter 4 and later in this chapter).

Where to start?

Assuming that a large proportion of the organization is to be covered, there are essentially three alternatives:

- the scattergun approach;

- the stepped approach;

- a combination of these.

The scattergun approach is to take jobs almost at random throughout the organization and to build up a complete picture gradually. The benefit of this approach is that no staff group appears to be favoured at any one time but the disadvantages are that it may take some time for sufficient jobs to be evaluated to allow meaningful moderation (see below) and it generally prolongs the programme.

The stepped approach is to identify separate staff groups (usually by department or location) and evaluate all jobs in the group before progressing to the next group. If one group that is keen to move ahead can be identified and handled first, this can set a standard for momentum and goodwill for the rest of the programme. To make best use of time, activities can overlap: eg fact gathering can have moved on to group 3 while evaluations are being carried out for group 2 and moderation/review is being handled for group 1. An example of an activity chart is given in Figure 10.1.

The combination approach is essentially the stepped approach but it recognizes that there is a need to evaluate key jobs throughout the organization at the start of the programme. These will normally be jobs with multiple jobholders in order to confirm that the provisional grade boundaries do not disadvantage any staff group (particularly not by gender) or to provide additional information so that implementation costs can be more accurately predicted.

How long will it take?

Having established the number of jobs to be evaluated, the overall time required will be almost directly related to the people resources that are made available – the more trained analysts, evaluators, etc available, the more quickly the work can be done. An extreme example of this is the introduction of a new system in the Health & Safety Executive in the early 1990s.

Activity	Month											
	1	2	3	4	5	6	7	8	9	10	11	12
Group 1												
– Information gathering	▬											
– Evaluation		▬										
– Review/moderation			▬									
Group 2												
– Information gathering			▬									
– Evaluation				▬								
– Review/moderation					▬							
Group 3												
– Information gathering					▬							
– Evaluation						▬						
– Review/moderation							▬					
Group 4												
– Information gathering							▬					
– Evaluation								▬				
– Review/moderation									▬			
Group 5												
– Information gathering									▬			
– Evaluation										▬		
– Review/moderation											▬	
Final Review												▬

Figure 10.1 Job evaluation programme activity chart

Case study: The HSE had been formed by the amalgamation of various 'Inspectorates' from different government departments, bringing with them over 130 different pay grades. A new system of evaluation, grading and pay needed to be developed and installed as quickly as possible.

With the full participation of the relevant unions, an HSE-specific factor plan was developed and tested and a version of the Gauge system built around this. The Gauge version was also thoroughly tested and both management and unions declared themselves satisfied that the system produced consistent and valid evaluation results.

Eighteen analysts were then fully trained in how to 'facilitate' an evaluation with a jobholder and line manager without pre-written job descriptions. Armed with 18 notebook PCs that had HSE-Gauge pre-installed, they evaluated over 2,000 jobs in less than three months. 'Appeals' were minimal, as the unions declared that they would only support a request for an evaluation review if jobholders could demonstrate that one or more of the answers given during the evaluation (which they were presumed to have agreed at the time) were incorrect.

Scheduling individual meetings

Each fact-gathering meeting, whether it be to prepare a job description, to complete a paper questionnaire or to answer computer-generated questions, will ideally involve at least three people – the jobholder, the line manager and the analyst – and take between one and two hours. This means that meetings have to be scheduled well in advance, particularly if they form a collection of meetings in one location. A month or more ahead is often needed in order to avoid holidays and business and other commitments. The principle must be established that, once set, meetings may not be cancelled except for emergencies. It is all too easy for job evaluation to be seen as a low priority and, if this is allowed to happen, the implementation plan and even the credibility of the system itself will be damaged.

Whether or not a staff representative should also attend these meetings is a matter for the organization to decide. If they do attend, it should be made clear that they are there as observers, making sure that the jobholder's input is respected, and not to take part in the actual evaluation.

The location for the meeting is important and, as the primary purpose is to establish accurate information about the job, it is best held at a location where the jobholder will feel at ease. A quiet, neutral location is best, away from all sources of interruption – the line manager's office is arguably the worst!

Date, time and location should be confirmed in writing (or e-mail) about a week in advance and, if not already issued in other communication, a briefing note about the purpose and conduct of the meeting should be sent (see Appendix 8 for an example).

Top-down, bottom-up or random?

A decision as to whether the more senior jobs or the more junior ones within a group should be evaluated first, or whether they should be selected at random, should be taken by the steering group and applied throughout the organization. There are arguments in favour of each of these approaches but, on balance, provided that the system has first been validated on 'test jobs' from all levels, the top-down approach is to be preferred for three reasons:

1. In each evaluation the line manager will have the benefit of previous experience through having been involved in the evaluation of his/her own job. This should lead to more objective input and guidance.

2. Each line manager should be better placed to ensure that the similarities and differences between the jobs for which he/she is directly responsible are properly identified and evaluated, particularly if these are dealt with in quick succession.

3. Perhaps cynically, line managers will be less inclined to encourage overstatement of subordinate jobs. (If the subordinate job is evaluated first, and higher than it merits, the manager's own job score could subsequently benefit from this.)

There is, of course, the alternate risk that some managers may attempt to understate the subordinate job in order to increase the relative difference between it and their own job.

EVALUATING JOBS

The way in which this, the central aspect of implementation, is carried out will vary according to which evaluation process the organization chooses to adopt.

Computer-based systems

For those organizations opting for one of the more advanced computerized evaluation systems, the information-gathering process discussed above should normally result directly in an automatic evaluation of the job. This is, in principle, the ideal approach, with the jobholder directly involved in the actual evaluation of his/her job.

Some of these organizations, however, may prefer to collect information from the jobholder and line manager in paper format and then have trained analysts answer the on-screen questions on their behalf. While this may reduce the risk of any 'collusion' between jobholder and line manager to provide inappropriate answers, it reintroduces a judgemental element by a third party. In some situations this could be seen as negating one of the main benefits of the computerized approach – its scoring consistency.

Paper-based systems

Those organizations opting for a traditional, paper-based process will need to have the collected information analysed and evaluated by one or more specialist analysts or, more normally, by a trained evaluation panel assembled for the purpose as described below.

Using job evaluation panels

If a panel is used, it is normal and highly desirable for the initial members to be the same as those involved in the evaluation of the 'test jobs' during the scheme development (see Chapter 7). However, a larger pool of potential panel members is usually required to reduce the workload on individuals (evaluation meetings may well cover several days) and allow for holidays and other commitments.

It is essential for the additional panel members to be trained very thoroughly in the factor and level definitions and, preferably, in their development. It is also desirable to provide them with 'hands on' experience in the actual evaluation of jobs before taking part in 'live' evaluations. A good way to achieve this is for the additional members to form a panel and evaluate a sample of the test jobs, observed by some of the original panel. Any differences in scores between the new panel and the original one provides the opportunity to explore the subtlety of interpretation that the original panel adopted and which the new members must adhere to if consistency of evaluation is to be maintained.

The actual evaluation process will differ from one organization to another but a number of principles should be adhered to:

1. No untrained person should be allowed to take part in, nor to influence, an evaluation.

2. All evaluators should have the input information at least a week prior to the evaluation meeting (to provide the opportunity to clarify anything that is unclear and thus save time at the meeting itself).

3. No aspect of the jobholder as a person should influence any aspect of the evaluation (specifically not gender or ethnic origin).

4. The evaluation is concerned with the normal content of the job as defined in a job description or role analysis. It should not be affected by the activities of any individuals which vary the standard job requirements.

5. A full record of the scoring decisions should be kept and the reasons why that level was determined noted (a rationale). This is particularly important if the panel found it difficult to reach consensus, as it may be relevant if a review of that evaluation is called for.

6. All evaluation scores should be treated as provisional (and not disclosed) until they have been reviewed by some other body (steering group, review panel or audit panel).

Panel workload

Job evaluation is quite hard work. The amount of time panel members can spend working effectively is fairly limited. The time taken to evaluate individual jobs will depend on the extent to which panel members find it difficult to carry out the evaluation and reach consensus. Some jobs will be quite straightforward and may take less than an hour to evaluate. Others are more complex or raise particular evaluation problems and can take as much as two or three hours.

However, as panels gain experience and become familiar with the factor plan and the job evaluation process, they can speed up their evaluations. They will have learnt more about relating job descriptions to factor level definitions, various 'conventions' on how particular aspects of jobs should be treated will have evolved and there will be a data bank (recorded but also in the memory of panel members) on how levels have been evaluated in comparable jobs.

There is something to be said for limiting meetings to a morning session if that is at all possible – panels can run out of steam in the afternoon. But in the initial stages this may mean that no more than two or three jobs will have been evaluated, although later on it should be possible to increase the number to, say, four or even five jobs. If this approach is impossible (because it would prolong the evaluation programme or because of difficulties in convening panel members), then whole-day sessions might have to be accepted. Off-site 'away days' for panels can work very well and an experienced panel can evaluate as many as 10 jobs in a single day.

Conducting job evaluation panel meetings

The choice of the person who chairs the panel and how the role is carried out are critical to the quality of, and respect accorded to, the panel's decisions. The chair should be someone with a good overview of the whole organization or an external consultant – someone who should be seen as having no 'hidden agenda' – with the skill and personal authority to chair and facilitate the meeting in a professional manner.

The chair has to agree with the panel how evaluations should be carried out. There is a choice of method. The best method is to get the panel to evaluate one factor at a time for all the jobs under consideration. The panel exchanges views about the factor evaluation and, under the guidance of the facilitator, reaches agreement. Experience has shown that this makes it easier to achieve consensus. An in-depth factor-by-factor approach rather than a job-by-job approach means that panel members are less likely to make decisions on total scores based on *a priori* judgements about the relative value of the whole jobs, which they might find it hard to change. They are more likely to focus on 'read-across' analytical judgements about the level of particular factors and it will be easier for them to refer for guidance to previous evaluations of the same factor in other benchmark jobs. It also takes less time than other methods because it is possible to concentrate on factor evaluations that are questionable relative to the levels given to other jobs. When there are variations in factor evaluations, individual panel members would be asked to give reasons for their conclusions. But the chair has to be careful not to allow them to be pressurized to change their views. If panel members have been properly trained and if there is a carefully designed, tested and understood factor plan and good information about the job, the extent to which evaluations vary is usually fairly limited, which enables consensus to be achieved more easily.

The alternative, but less desirable method is to get each member to evaluate whole jobs factor by factor and then to inform the panel of their conclusions. The chair records their separate views and then initiates a discussion with the objective of achieving consensus on the rating for each factor and therefore the overall score. This can be time consuming because panel members may be influenced by pre-formed judgements and, having made up their minds, find it diffi-cult to shift their ground.

A variation of this approach is to get each panel member to study the whole job to form an opinion about how each factor in the job should be evaluated but not to communicate their views formally to other members of the panel. Instead, the panel as a whole, with facilitation from the chair, discusses and agrees (if at all possible) the evaluation of each factor in turn to produce a total job evaluation score. This speeds up the evaluation and experience has shown that consensus can be easier to achieve because panel members are not put in the position of having to defend their prior judgements against all comers. But there is the danger of the weaker members of the panel allowing themselves to be swayed by strongly expressed majority views. This approach therefore only works with good facilitation which ensures that the discussion is not dominat-ed by one or two powerful members and that all members have their say. Some organizations start with the first approach and move on to the second one when panel members (and the facilita-tor) become more experienced.

Good facilitation is crucial and the overall responsibility of the chair should be to facilitate the discussion and obtain consensus on the evaluation. In particular, the chair should:

- make sure that the panel is well balanced and that everyone understands that all members have an equal say in the deliberations and decision making;

▮ lay down the ground rules for evaluation and agree the methodology;

▮ ensure that each job is fully understood (through examination of job information and round-table discussion) before any evaluation is attempted; the chair should have the authority to suspend an evaluation if the available information appears to be incomplete or misleading;

▮ initiate the discussion on each factor if a factor-by-factor approach is used;

▮ guide panel members through the evaluation, probing where necessary to test whether views have been properly justified on the basis of the evidence, but not giving any indication of the chair's own views – it is the panel members who carry out the evaluation, not the chair;

▮ continually reinforce the principles that it is the job and not the performance of the person that is being evaluated and the need to avoid gender or other bias;

▮ remind panel members that it is the job content as it is intended to be carried out that is evaluated, not the job as carried out by a particular jobholder;

▮ actively encourage the participation of every panel member;

▮ as a facilitator, stimulate reasoned debate;

▮ ensure that people respect alternative views and, where appropriate, are prepared to change their initial stance when presented with a valid reason to do so;

▮ bear in mind that a lone voice may have a significant contribution to make; dissenters should therefore be given a reasonable chance to express their view subject to them not being allowed to dominate the discussion – most seasoned panel members will be able to recall at least one '12 Angry

Men' situation where a presumed consensus for the 'obvious' conclusion was overturned by one person's persistence;

▌ be alert to, and suppress, any factions or cliques developing in the panel – one approach might be to change the seating plan each session;

▌ ensure that the consensus reached is not a 'false consensus' (one for which there is no dissenting voice only because one or more dissenters are too afraid to speak out against more dominant members) – it will be up to the chair to be particularly sensitive to this and deliberately to encourage the more reticent members to state their views;

▌ be scrupulously neutral at all times – to achieve this, chairs normally do not carry out any evaluations themselves but in their facilitator role they can when necessary challenge (gently) panel members to justify their views, press for discussion based on the evidence rather than opinion and bring to the attention of panel members any evidence or relevant facts that will help them to reach an agreed conclusion;

▌ ensure that the decisions of the panel and their rationale are recorded – the latter is important if at a later stage a review of the evaluation is called for;

▌ if the panel is unable to reach a true consensus within a reasonable time, the chair should not try to force the issue but should have the authority to put the job to one side for further reflection or so that more information about the point at issue can be obtained;

▌ as a last resort, chairs have been known to put panels to the vote, but this is undesirable because it divides the panel – consensus may be difficult to attain but experience has shown that it can always be achieved, although this may take time.

The outcomes of the panel's deliberations should be treated as provisional until it is reviewed (see below).

Job 'slotting' and equal pay considerations

It has been (and still is) common practice, particularly in larger organizations, to evaluate only a limited sample of jobs and to refer to these as 'benchmark jobs'. Other jobs are then 'slotted' into appropriate grades through some form of whole-job comparison against these benchmarks.

Even if this 'slotting' is carried out by the trained evaluation panel, and every jobholder is subsequently given the right to ask for his/her slotted job to be re-evaluated using the full factor analysis process, this still would not provide a defence against an equal pay claim if it is done on a 'whole job' basis rather than analytically, factor by factor. The reason is that some jobs (more likely to be 'male jobs') may get slotted too high and the holders of these jobs will be most unlikely to ask for a full evaluation. As they would not have been 'analysed and evaluated under the scheme in question', the 'job evaluation study' defence would not cover them and any claim using one of these as the comparator job would almost certainly be permitted by an Employment Tribunal.

This can have significant implications on the number of jobs that have to be evaluated and hence the total implementation time. In large organizations it would be unrealistic to attempt to evaluate every job but, by inference, every jobholder must 'sign off' a full evaluation that he/she is prepared to accept as applying to his/her job.

The use of 'generic' role profiles is one approach to this problem. Another is to use the 'copy' facility available in most computerized systems, in which an exact copy of a relevant original evaluation can be made, including all the original answers, and jobholders invited to identify any questions that they would have answered differently. These, and only these, questions can then be answered afresh by the new jobholder, creating a unique evaluation for that job in a much shorter time and retaining the consistency with the original (different answers would have to be fully justified before acceptance).

REVIEW OF RESULTS

All evaluations, whether resulting from a paper-based approach as in the preceding section or from a computer-aided process, should be subject to review before the grading structure is designed and information on gradings is disclosed to jobholders and their line managers. This is to ensure, as far as possible, that no questionable outcomes are revealed without first being cross-checked.

Evaluations should normally be regarded as provisional until all requests for review have been dealt with, as a resultant change to one evaluation may impact on other jobs for which no reviews have been requested (see below). If this is likely to create unacceptable delay between the evaluation itself and the notification of outcome, evaluations may have to be grouped (eg by location, function or job family) and review requests that are based on comparisons with other jobs only allowed within the group concerned.

It must also be recognized that, deliberately or otherwise, some people may provide misleading or incorrect information to the evaluation process that is not identified as such. This may produce an inappropriate grading that, if published, could affect people's perception of the evaluation scheme itself.

The initial evaluation results and subsequent gradings must also be monitored for their impact on male- and female-dominated jobs. A new job evaluation scheme may well result in some upward movement of female-dominated jobs as historical gender bias is eliminated.

Paper-based systems

If a very experienced panel has carried out the evaluations with plenty of previously approved evaluations to refer to, this review can be carried out quite quickly. It could even be conducted by the head of job evaluation, the HR manager or someone else in a similar position. That person should not have been a member of the panel that carried out the evaluations but must have a good 'feel' for the emerging relativities of jobs. Possible anomalous results, shown up by comparison with earlier evaluations, should be checked but the panel's decisions should normally be respected. The panel itself should have been alert to potentially misleading information and either ignored it or asked for further proof of its validity.

While the implementation is still in its early stages, however, the panel will have relatively few previous, confirmed evaluations to refer to and will be establishing new reference points for the future. A careful check by another body can avoid mistakes going unrectified and inappropriate standards set, and can also reduce the number of later requests for reviews from jobholders.

Computer-aided systems

As outlined in Chapter 8, one of the advantages of the more sophisticated computer-aided systems is that there is no need for evaluation panels, the equivalent of panel judgements being built in to the system rules or logic. This does mean, however, that there is a greater possibility of misleading or incorrect job information being unrecognized and affecting the job score, even with system checks in place for unusual score profiles. Computer output can be credited with spurious validity and a review by a small panel, trained to look for anomalies and to query input information, is essential.

The review process

The outcome of the evaluation programme should be reviewed by a small panel of experienced evaluators who have a good 'feel' for the organization as a whole. Its role is to examine the rank order of jobs resulting from the completed evaluations and to look for any results that seem out of place. In doing this, the panel must ensure that it is not being influenced by any desire to maintain previous, possibly incorrect, relativities.

This process will usually start with an examination of the rank order of jobs based on their total weighted points, but should not be restricted to this. As with the checking of 'test job' scores (see Chapter 7), a more objective way to review results is to examine the rank order of jobs within each factor, eg:

▓ An unexpected score in a 'knowledge' or 'expertise' factor could indicate a score more related to the jobholder's personal qualifications than to the job requirements.

▌ A score in any 'responsibility' or 'authority' factor that is the same as (or higher than) that of the line manager would normally be inappropriate (another reason to prefer the top-down sequencing of evaluations).

▌ A factor level that is different from that awarded to the nearest relevant test job or similar, previously evaluated job could indicate misleading input information.

The review panel should have available to it all the input information that gave rise to the evaluation scores, together with any notes made during the evaluation itself (the rationale). It should also have the authority to call for additional information if required, from any source. The panel should not, of itself, change evaluation scores but should return those jobs whose evaluation appears questionable to the original evaluation group, with a clear note of what should be rechecked and why.

DISCLOSURE OF RESULTS

There are no 'right' answers to the questions often posed regarding how much information about evaluation results should be made known to whom and when. Practice varies greatly from one organization to another and current practice may be the best guide. It is normal for organizations to let people know which grade their job is in and, usually, which other jobs are also in that grade (restricted to their own job family or group if the organization is large). Many organizations release details of the whole grade structure. While the grading of posts resulting from job evaluation must be communicated to all concerned, the case for releasing the job evaluation scores supporting the gradings is not so clear cut.

In principle, if the system is to be truly open and transparent then all details of the evaluation scores for jobs should be made known to anyone who has the right to ask for them. If such details are not disclosed it may lead to mistrust in the objectivity and fairness of the system ('what are they trying to hide?'). It is all too easy, however, for people who have not been trained in job evaluation to misunderstand or misinterpret such detailed information and this level of openness may create more difficulties than it solves. When considering this issue, it should be remembered that the evaluation has been carried out by a trained panel of evaluators or reviewed by such a panel. They are the only ones that fully understand the process. If the panel includes staff representatives, as it should do, then this, coupled with a full communication programme, should help to create a climate of trust in the system.

Jobholders

All jobholders whose jobs have been evaluated should be told how this will affect their grading and what effect this will have on their pay before any change to pay arrangements is implemented. The best way to disseminate this information is through the line manager (see below).

Line managers

In addition to information on their own jobs, line managers should be told the grades of all jobs for which they are responsible (both directly and through others). Without this, managers cannot be expected to share responsibility (with HR) for the overall job evaluation and grading programme, nor to fulfil two of their key roles in it which are: 1) to carry out a final check to identify possible grading errors; and 2) to act as the first assessor of any review request from a jobholder.

In the first of these the manager should take a proactive role, checking if any of the proposed grades are (in his/her view) inappropriate and asking for a review of those evaluations. The manager's perception will, inevitably, be that of an 'untrained' (possibly subjective or biased) person and should be treated as such, but the pragmatic view may prevent mistakes being made public.

This responsibility has already been referred to earlier in this chapter as one of the arguments in favour of the 'top-down' sequencing of evaluations. Line managers should accept the grading before they pass them on to the jobholders themselves. This makes it clear that the grading of jobs is the concern of line managers and not an HR-imposed ideology.

If the above approach is followed, line managers become the natural first assessor for any review request. They will have implicitly 'approved' the results for all subordinate jobs and, if the request is unjustified, should be in a position to explain why and convince the jobholder that this is so. If, however, the jobholder can demonstrate that something has been overlooked or misinterpreted, managers will be in a position to forward the review request with their full backing. If the manager does not support the request, it must still be forwarded if the jobholder insists, but with an explanation of why it is not supported.

Evaluation panel, review panel, staff representatives

Each of these should have access, in confidence, to any aspect of the evaluation and grading of those jobs for which they have a responsibility.

REVIEWING THE EVALUATION OR GRADING OF A JOB

There are essentially two situations where a review of the evaluation or grading of a job might properly be requested: 1) when the job is first allocated a grade and that grade is made known to the parties concerned; 2) when the content of a job changes (or is about to change) sufficiently to place doubt on the existing grading of that job.

Requests arising under the first of these situations are best referred to as 'evaluation reviews' (a less confrontational term than 'appeals' and therefore preferable); requests arising under the second situation should be referred to as 're-evaluations' and are covered in the next chapter.

It is often assumed that only the jobholder(s) concerned can request a review of the grading of a job. In principle, however, to ensure that possible over-gradings as well as under-gradings can be checked, any of the following should be able to do so:

- *jobholders* – because they believe that some aspect of the job was wrongly assessed or because they think a very similar job has been graded differently;

- *line managers* – because they believe that some aspect of the job was wrongly assessed, because another similar job for which they are responsible has been graded differently or because this job has been graded the same as one that is substantially different;

▪ *other people doing the same job* – because they believe that the original evaluation does not correctly cover the main demands or responsibilities of their job, even though the jobs have been declared to be broadly the same and the grading to apply to both.

The best way to minimize the number of requests for reviews is, of course, to put in the necessary investment in time and training at all stages of the system development, testing and implementation, in particular making sure that the input information is accurate and agreed.

A formal evaluation review procedure should be prepared, agreed and issued before any evaluation results are made known. It would normally only set out the procedure to be followed by a jobholder but it is usually worthwhile stating in the introduction to the procedure that each of the categories of people above have the right to ask for a review for the reasons given. The procedure to be followed by a jobholder will depend on the evaluation process used (computerized systems only justify reviews based on matters of fact) but should normally include the following steps:

1. Discuss the areas of concern with the line manager to establish whether or not he/she is prepared to support a request for a re-evaluation. If not, the request should go no further unless the jobholder feels sufficiently strongly to insist on the appeal going forward.

2. If the line manager supports the request, he/she should prepare a brief note to whoever is responsible for the job evaluation programme (the JE manager), explaining the reason for the request and providing supporting evidence.

3. If a request goes forward against the line manager's advice, the jobholder and manager should submit separate notes stating their cases (with supporting evidence).

4. The JE manager should examine the request, add his/her own notes and arrange for it to go before the review panel, together with all available details of the original evaluation. If the request is based on a comparison with another job, details of that evaluation should also be assembled.

5. The review panel should examine all documents and decide whether a re-evaluation is justified. If the request is based on the claim that job information has been misinterpreted rather than on matters of fact (manual systems only), the panel should try to establish why this was not identified during the original evaluation or review.

6. If the review panel believes that a request based on a comparison with another job is potentially valid but that it is the comparator job that was wrongly evaluated, it should present both jobs for re-evaluation.

7. The re-evaluation process should be the same as for the original evaluation but focusing only on the issues raised in stages 1 to 6 above.

8. The result of the re-evaluation should be submitted to the review panel for approval and there should be no further appeal against that panel's decision.

It is normal to put a time limit on any request that is based on errors of fact or mis-evaluation. Two weeks is a common maximum period. Many, if not most, requests are, however, based on a comparison with other evaluations, as that is the only practical way that job-holders (and even line managers) have of assessing whether or not jobs have been fairly graded. If the issuing of (provisional) grading results for jobs that fall within the same part of the organization is spread over a long period, requests based on other evaluations will have to be allowed past the end of that period.

If a jobholder is dissatisfied with the review panel's decision, he/she is normally given the right to appeal, which would be dealt with under the standard grievance procedure of the organization.

FINALIZING PAY RANGES

As part of the overall system development, grade and pay ranges will have been developed as described in Chapter 9. It may, however, be prudent to delay the finalization of grade boundaries and pay ranges until the majority of jobs have been evaluated, particularly the heavily populated ones, to avoid any potential equal pay issues which may arise if large numbers of female-populated jobs are placed just below a grade boundary or large numbers of male-populated ones are placed just above. It also provides the opportunity to ensure that the inevitable short-term increase in the pay bill is acceptable to the organization.

This increase is inevitable because there are bound to be some jobs where the jobholder's pay is below the minimum rate for the job's new grade and it is universally accepted that it is good practice not to allow anyone to be underpaid in these circumstances, although the required increase to the minimum rate for the employee's revised grade may be phased for financial reasons (if that happens, employees are said to have been 'green circled'). The converse, where the current jobholder's pay is greater than the maximum for the job's new grade and they are 'red circled', cannot be used to offset the costs arising from redressing underpayments as it would be highly unusual (and possibly illegal) to reduce anyone's pay in this circumstance.

The cost of assimilation

The total short-term, or 'assimilation', cost will depend on many factors, chief of which are:

- whether or not the organization had an objective and well-managed pay structure prior to the job evaluation exercise;

- the extent to which the organization had achieved the principles of equal value in the past;

- the extent to which the new grade and pay structure is a radical departure from what existed and its introduction has therefore created many anomalies;

▌ the planned assimilation policy.

As already noted, this assimilation cost should have been estimated and accepted (by the organization) before the full implementation programme was initiated. As noted above, the costs will vary according to circumstances but as a rule of thumb based on the empirical evidence of recent evaluation exercises the cost can be between 2 and 4 per cent of the pay bill (if there are no major changes to the rank order). However, if in the final analysis, the assimilation cost is likely to be unacceptably greater than this, an appropriate assimilation policy as described below may help to overcome the difficulty.

PAY ASSIMILATION AND PROTECTION

While it is best to keep discussions on job evaluation and pay totally separate, dealing with the outcomes of a job evaluation exercise and their impact on people's pay and organization costs is often the most difficult part of the implementation process. The issues are: 1) where to assimilate staff on their new pay range; 2) how to deal with people whose pay is below or above the pay for their new grade, and 3) what policies should be adopted to 'protect' the pay of those who are overpaid in relation to their grade and have been red circled.

Assimilation policy

There are essentially four categories of staff to be covered by the assimilation policy:

▌ those staff whose current actual pay and pay potential are both encompassed by the pay range for the new grades to which their jobs are allocated;

▌ those staff whose current pay lies within the new pay range but whose existing pay potential is greater than the new maximum;

▌ those staff whose current pay is below the minimum for the new grade;

▌ those staff whose current pay is above the maximum for the new grade.

Current pay and pay potential both within the new pay range

In some ways this group is the easiest to deal with and the majority of staff will normally be included in it. The only point at issue is whether or not any increase should be awarded on transition and the answer should be 'no'. The only exception would normally be if pay levels within the new ranges are to be on fixed points only (the 'pay spine' approach described in Chapter 9) when the policy would normally be to move each person's pay to the nearest higher pay point.

Good advance communications should have conveyed the fact that job evaluation does not necessarily mean any increase in pay. But some people in this group may still feel disadvantaged at seeing others getting increases. This negative reaction can be decreased by introducing the new structure at the same time as any annual pay increase, so that everyone gets at least something.

It is necessary to be aware of the possibility of creating equal pay problems when assimilating staff to their new scale. For example, if two people with broadly equivalent experience and skills are on different current salaries and are assimilated into the same new grade but at the different salaries as determined by their previous salaries, it would appear that there is no equal pay problem – they are both on the same grade with the same grade and salary potential. But an equal value issue is only avoided if a lower paid man or woman has the opportunity to catch up with the higher paid man or woman within a reasonable period (say three or four years). However, where the difference was nothing to do with grade in the first place and can be shown to be unsustainable now that the jobs are graded equally, an uplift in pay is required. In these circumstances the higher paid individual may be red circled and have their pay protected as suggested below. Any such salary uplifts should be reviewed and implemented only after the jobs are first assimilated into the new scales and the costs of doing so confirmed. It would be wrong to saddle the new job evaluation and grade system with the costs of rectifying past discriminatory practices.

Current pay within the new pay range but pay potential higher than new maximum

No immediate increase is necessary in this circumstance but employees should be told what will happen. If progression to the old maximum was based on service only, ie automatic annual increases to the maximum, this guarantee will have to be retained. However, once a person's pay passes the maximum for the grade, this will then become a 'red circle' situation and should be treated as such (see below).

If progression to the old maximum was not guaranteed, but was based on performance, competencies etc, then the range maximum should normally be applied. Care will be needed to ensure that this does not adversely affect any specific category of staff, particularly female staff.

Current pay below the minimum for the new grade

Both justice and equity demand that, if someone has now been identified as being underpaid, the situation should be rectified as quickly as possible. Correcting this situation, by raising the pay to the minimum of the new pay range, should normally be the first call on any money allocated to the assimilation process. Each case should, however, be taken on its merits. If someone has recently been appointed to a post and given a pay increase at that time, it may be appropriate to wait until that person has completed a pro-bationary period before awarding another pay increase.

If the total cost of rectifying underpayments is more than the organization can afford, it may be necessary, however unpalatable, to phase the necessary increases, say one portion in the current year and the rest next year – it is undesirable to phase increases over a longer period unless the circumstances are exceptional. The simplest approach is to place a maximum on the increase that any one person may receive. This can be in absolute terms (eg maximum of £2,000) or in percentage increase terms (eg, maximum of 20 per cent of current pay). Another alternative is to use an annual 'gap reduction' approach (eg pay increase of 50 per cent of the difference between current pay and range minimum or £500, whichever is the greater).

Again, if any delay in rectifying underpayment situations is necessary and some staff have therefore to be 'green circled', it must not disadvantage one staff group more than another. Most organizations introducing job evaluation for the first time (or replacing an outdated scheme) will find that more women than men have to be green circled. Failure to correct these would be a perpetuation of gender bias.

Current pay above the maximum for the new grade

These situations which lead to red circling are usually the most difficult to deal with. They normally include a high proportion of people (often male) who have been in their current job a long time and who have been able to benefit from a lax approach to pay management in the past. People can take very different attitudes about what should be done about these situations and, as a result, the most protracted of the implementation negotiations are often centred on 'how to handle the red circles'.

At one end of the scale is the argument that these people are now known to be receiving more pay than the job is worth and that this should be stopped as soon as possible, especially if the organization needs that money to pay more to those people who have been (or are still) receiving less than they should. The opposite stance is that these people have become accustomed to a standard of living based on the pay that the organization has been willing to provide up to now and they should not suffer just because new standards are being applied. This is the principle that is usually adopted but there are different ways of applying it.

Any assimilation policy must set out how the 'red circle' situations will be handled. The starting point is normally that no one should suffer a reduction in pay – it should be 'protected' or 'safeguarded'. Thereafter, it is a matter of how quickly pay can and should be brought in line. Approaches to protection are discussed below.

Protection policies

'Indefinite protection', that is, maintaining the difference between current pay and range maximum for as long as the employee remains in the job, is highly undesirable. First, because it will create permanent anomalies, and second, because, where there are a lot of men in this situation (which is often the case), it will perpetuate unacceptable gender gaps. The Equal Opportunities Commission in its Good Practice Guide on Job Evaluation Schemes Free of Sex Bias states that red circling 'should not be used on such a scale that it amounts to sex discrimination'. And as stated by the Equal Pay Task Force: 'The use of red or green circling which maintains a difference in pay between men and women over more than a phase-in period of time will be difficult to justify.'

Because of these considerations, the most common approach now is to provide for red-circled employees to receive any across-the-board (cost of living) increase awarded to staff generally for a protection period which is usually limited to two to three years. They will no longer be entitled to general increases after the time limit has been reached until their rate of pay falls within the new scale for their job. They will then be entitled to the same increases as any other staff in their grade up to the grade maximum. If a red-circled individual concerned leaves the job, the scale of pay for the job reverts to the standard range as set up following job evaluation. Where there is an incremental pay structure, it is usual to allow staff to continue to earn any increments to which they are entitled under existing arrangements, up to the maximum of their present scale.

If there is no limit to the protection period, red-circled staff continue to be eligible for general increases for as long as they remain in their present job. They are then on what is sometimes called a 'personal to jobholder' scale.

Throughout the protection period, and particularly at the start of it, every attempt should be made to resolve the 'red circle' cases by other means. If jobholders are thought to be worth the current salary, then they may well be underused in their existing job. Attempts should be made to resolve this by either: a) increasing the job responsibilities so that the job will justify regrading to a higher grade, or b) moving the person concerned to a higher graded job as soon as an appropriate vacancy arises.

ENSURING EQUAL VALUE

To ensure equal value considerations are fully taken into account, it is essential throughout the programme to ensure that all significant features of jobs carried out by women as well as those undertaken by men are first 'captured' as part of the process, and then fairly evaluated.

11

Managing job evaluation

Many organizations heave a collective sigh of relief once the final job has been evaluated and graded and the last pay anomaly dealt with, assuming that job evaluation can now be put to one side. It is not like that!

Other organizations fear that a job evaluation programme is like 'painting the Forth Bridge' – as soon as you have got to the end you have to start again at the beginning. This inference of an inevitable, perpetual grind of evaluations is also wrong.

The Forth Bridge analogy is, however, relevant if looked at in the right way. The more thorough the preparation, the more care with which the materials are chosen and the more attention paid to their application, the longer it will be before any repainting is required. Regular inspection should identify those spots where things are getting flaky and prompt action should prevent the problem spreading. Some areas protected from the elements will last almost indefinitely while other areas will need continual touching-up. The use of new technology will ensure better coverage and adapting the paint composition to meet changing conditions should mean that a total repaint will not be necessary for a very long time.

Managing job evaluation is very like that and it is worth repeating here the summary of respondent views from the E-Reward survey quoted in Chapter 3:

The advice given by respondents on maintaining job evaluation is to hold regular reviews of scheme effectiveness, maintain adequate training for those operating the scheme, use IT in a smarter way, maintain ongoing communication, achieve more line accountability and involvement.

This closing chapter focuses on that advice but starts with the more mundane routines required to keep current evaluations up to date.

ANNUAL INDIVIDUAL EVALUATION/GRADING CHECKS

While the content of some jobs often changes in an obvious, stepped fashion, many jobs evolve or develop gradually. Over time, the effect of these changes can become significant and, while some jobholders will be alert to the re-evaluation opportunities this might present, others (often women) may be more modest. It is thus important that there is a mechanism to ensure that the cumulative effects of all such incremental changes are recognized at the appropriate time, to prevent any risk of creeping gender (or any other) bias in the system.

In those organizations that have annual performance/development review meetings between managers and their individual team members, this can be done by including a check on the current validity of all material relating to the evaluation of the job. If both parties agree that the job has changed in some significant way since it was last evaluated, a re-evaluation request can be initiated (see below).

This review of job evaluation data can also be useful in focusing the performance discussion on those aspects of the job demands that gave rise to the higher factor scores (ie the more important aspects of the job), minimizing the time spent on those of the jobholder's skills that are not relevant to the job or, alternatively, helping to identify skills that are currently underused.

If the organization does not require managers to carry out periodic performance reviews with their staff, as part of the pay review process they should be required to report on the current validity of job grades at least once every two years. The selection of jobs put forward for re-evaluation should be checked carefully for any gender bias to avoid the risk noted above.

Re-evaluation requests

During the implementation phase of a job evaluation programme (see Chapter 10), the provisional evaluation or grading of any job may be reviewed on request. Such requests will normally be based on the premise that the job demands were incorrectly assessed during the original evaluation. In some instances, the request will be based on the assertion that the input information was incorrect or incomplete.

Once the implementation phase is complete, however, the only reason for a re-evaluation should be that the job itself has changed. The people entitled to submit a re-evaluation request should be the jobholder or line manager, preferably through a joint submission.

A procedure for this, accompanied by policy guidelines, should be developed and circulated. This should include guidance on how the changes from the original job demands can be described and a form may be designed for this purpose. Supporting evidence should be attached to any request for re-evaluation. It should be made clear in the policy guidelines that a change of duties is not sufficient reason unless the new ones make significantly higher demands on the jobholder in such terms as the level of responsibility and the knowledge and skills required.

When a re-evaluation request is submitted, it should be put through the same re-evaluation process as used for reviews during the implementation programme and the review should be carried out by equally well-trained and experienced people. Those carrying out the re-evaluation should have access to all the original evaluation records, including the rationale, and should satisfy themselves that a substantial change has occurred before changing any factor score. In the absence of compelling evidence, a 'no change' decision should be the norm. Any impression that 'softer' standards are applied during a re-evaluation will quickly lead to a flood of requests and, inevitably, grade drift.

The HR department should also be alert to the situation where the increase in responsibilities is temporary. Re-evaluation should only take place when a permanent change has taken place and this change is justified in terms of what the jobholder will be expected to achieve. Managers have been known to connive with jobholders to add temporary or unnecessary duties to the job description in order to inflate the grade. (This may appear to be a cynical point of view but in the experience of one of the writers of this book, managers are just as likely as jobholders to talk up jobs either to curry favour with the jobholders or to inflate the importance of their own job.) If significant activities have been permanently transferred from one job to another then both jobs will need to be re-evaluated.

One of the advantages of most computerized systems is that each factor score is the result of specific answers to specific questions. When a re-evaluation request is submitted, the record of original answers given (or the Job Overview in the case of Gauge) can be issued to the originators of the request, with the requirement for them to identify the question(s) that would now be answered differently and to provide the evidence for this new answer. If this evidence is not convincing, the original answer should stand.

SUGGESTIONS FROM PRACTITIONERS ON MANAGING JOB EVALUATION

'Regular reviews of scheme effectiveness'

All organizations are continually evolving, some more quickly than others. No matter how carefully the new job evaluation scheme has been developed, it can only be totally 'right' for the organization at the time of its development. Without regular review and retuning when necessary, it will gradually become viewed as 'yesterday's scheme', no longer valid for evaluating jobs in 'today's environment'. This risk was highlighted as one of the quoted 'cases against job evaluation' in Chapter 1.

The review need not be time consuming but it should be carried out on a regular basis which it is best to determine at the outset. It is usually worth scheduling the first, brief, review to take place approximately 12 months after the implementation programme has been completed. This should provide sufficient time for any final difficulties with the scheme to emerge and be corrected. Thereafter reviews should be carried out approximately every three to four years, although the optimum frequency will depend on the rate of change in the organization, the sector in which it operates or the technology it uses. A substantial step-change in any of these could prompt the need for a review before the due date.

A small, joint review team should be set up specifically to carry out the review and it may be best to give it a very broad remit, eg 'Examine and report on the validity of the existing job evaluation system for use over the next three to four years.' A useful start point could be to examine the reasons for, and the outcomes of, all re-evaluation requests (see above) that have been submitted over the previous three months. Any common features could point to aspects of the scheme that may need updating.

An increasing proportion of jobs scoring at the highest level in any factor could indicate the need for an additional level in that factor and a bulking (or thinning) of jobs in one of the middle levels may suggest that minor wording changes are required to redress the original balance across the levels.

If the organization deliberately and publicly changes from being a product-led business to a customer-led one, or from a finance-based one to a market-based one, a change in factor weightings may be indicated. In practice, such a change would normally have only marginal impact on job ranking but explaining the reasons for the change to staff is a powerful way to reinforce the new corporate philosophy. Changing weightings can, however, impact on job grades if the overall effect is to increase (or decrease) average job scores. All the cautions about checking the gender effect of this apply once more.

Any terminology or jargon used in the scheme should be kept up to date. If, for example, the organization has changed its name, or replaced 'division' with 'department' or 'profit centre', it is essential that the job evaluation scheme quickly reflects those changes. Even more important is the need to keep financial figures updated if these affect factor levels.

Large organizations with multiple copies of a paper-based scheme spread over many geographic locations are, naturally, more reluctant than others to update their schemes and are thus more likely to find their schemes being perceived as out of date. They also run the greatest risk of different versions of the scheme being used in different parts of the organization. Computerized schemes lend themselves to instantaneous, organization-wide updating, with no risk of old versions being used and a minimum of waste paper!

'Maintain adequate training'

As noted in Chapter 10, 'refresher' training for all those involved in the ongoing application of job evaluation should take place on a regular basis, to ensure that the original principles and standards are adhered to.

When new people are brought in to fulfil one of the roles, as will inevitably happen, they need to be given the full initial training first. This must include training in the avoidance of gender bias. Ideally, they should attend one of the refresher training sessions with 'seasoned' practitioners before first taking up their role, so that they can absorb any 'custom and practice' that has evolved and thus ensure that consistency is maintained.

People appointed as managers for the first time should be trained in the role they are expected to play in the ongoing maintenance of correct grades.

'Use IT in a smarter way'

All employees are becoming progressively more IT literate and the use of PCs is a part of everyday work for most people. Management information systems abound, virtually all software-based.

Ignoring all the other benefits that computer-based job evaluation systems can deliver (see Chapter 8), the impression that the HR department is in the forefront of IT technology is likely to do far more good than harm to its own image and to the respect with which its advice, support and decisions are received. Labouring away with 'old-fashioned' technology and burdening managers with time-consuming bureaucracy and paper is not the best way to gain their very necessary support (see below).

While there are many good reasons for developing and testing a new job evaluation scheme in the traditional manner, taking advantage of all the opportunities for involvement and discussion, large organizations in particular should be looking to computerize their schemes if they have not already done so. This can be done at the end of initial testing, at the end of the implementation phase or at any time during the life of the scheme, particularly at a major scheme review.

'Maintain ongoing communication'

The need for regular communication reduces significantly once job evaluation has been fully implemented throughout the organization but it should not cease totally. The nature, frequency, method and style of the communication should be in line with that already adopted for other HR-initiated communications and a regular item in the staff magazine can be a good vehicle. This could take the form of queries and answers (the queries being 'planted' if necessary in order to get a point across). The 'help line' number should be repeated regularly.

Changes to the composition of review panels should be publicized to remind staff that it is their own colleagues who make these important decisions, not the HR department in isolation. Any modifications to the scheme design or the evaluation process must be communicated and, if more than cosmetic, an open-forum session for interested or affected staff should be arranged.

All new staff should have the job evaluation and grading system described to them as a major item in their induction programme, and be encouraged to get their new manager to explain how the grading of their own job was arrived at.

'Achieve more line accountability and involvement'

The principle that the HR function should be a service to management and not an end in itself is nowhere more true than in job evaluation. The fact that this has often not been the case in the past, particularly in large organizations using complex schemes with unintelligible language that can only be understood by highly trained specialists, has been one of the main reasons for job evaluation's negative image. As noted in Chapter 1: 'Essentially, the case against job evaluation is that it is bureaucratic, inflexible, time consuming and inappropriate in today's organizations. It was this perception of job evaluation that led to it becoming discredited in many organizations in the late 1980s and early 1990s.'

The organizations that get real benefit from their job evaluation systems are those that ensure maximum 'ownership' by line managers of the evaluation outcomes. This can only realistically be obtained when managers:

- fully understand the evaluation system (including all gender issues) and have been involved in the evaluation process;

- have the opportunity to query any provisional gradings of the jobs for which they are responsible;

- have then accepted and taken responsibility for informing their staff of the gradings of their jobs and, if necessary, defended those gradings without reference to the HR department;

- accept their responsibility to keep these gradings up to date, supporting requests for re-evaluation by their staff when the request is justified and discouraging those that are not.

As stated in Chapter 10, the aim should be to make it clear that the evaluation and grading of jobs is part of the managerial process, not an HR-imposed ideology.

The less the situation conforms to the above ideal, the more likely it will be that managers abdicate their responsibilities to their staff, hiding behind an attitude of 'don't blame me, blame the HR evaluators'. Managers then start attempting to manipulate the scheme, and once this happens the scheme is doomed to eventual decay.

Earning management (and staff) support should be the aim and the reward will be a respected, smooth-running and long-lasting system.

Appendix 1

A job evaluation scheme designed to comply with equal value principles: the local government NJC job evaluation scheme factor plan

Factor/ Level	1	2	3	4	5	6	7	8	Total	% of total
1. Knowledge	20	40	60	80	100	121	142	163	163	16.3
2. Mental skills	13	26	39	52	65	78			78	7.8
3. Interpersonal skills	13	26	39	52	65	78			78	7.8
4. Physical skills	13	26	39	52	65				65	6.5
Knowledge and skills factors									384	38.4
5. Initiative and independence	13	26	39	52	65	78	91	104	104	10.4
6. Physical demands	10	20	30	40	50				50	5.0
7. Mental demands	10	20	30	40	50				50	5.0
8. Emotional demands	10	20	30	40	50				50	5.0
Effort factors									254	25.4
9. Responsibility for people	13	26	39	52	65	78			78	7.8
10. Responsibility for supervision	13	26	39	52	65	78			78	7.8
11. Responsibility for financial resources	13	26	39	52	65	78			78	7.8
12. Responsibility for physical resources	13	26	39	52	65	78			78	7.8
Responsibility factors									312	31.2
13. Working conditions	10	20	30	40	50				50	5.0
Environment factors									50	5.0
TOTAL									1000	100.0

Appendix 2

Suggested equal pay policy: the Equal Opportunities Commission

EQUAL PAY STATEMENT

This organization supports the principle of equal opportunities in employment and believes that as part of that principle male and female staff should receive equal pay for the same or broadly similar work, for work rated as equivalent and for work of equal value.

We understand that a right to equal pay between men and women free of sex bias is a fundamental principle of European Community law and is conferred by United Kingdom legislation.

We believe it is in our company's interest and good business practice that pay is awarded fairly and equitably.

We recognize that in order to achieve equal pay for employees doing equal work we should operate a pay system which is transparent, based on objective criteria and free from sex bias.

ACTION TO IMPLEMENT POLICY

In order to put our commitment to equal pay into practice we will:

▌ examine our existing and future pay practices for all our employees, including those in non-standard employment and those who are absent on pregnancy or maternity leave;

▌ carry out regular monitoring of the impact of our practices;

▌ inform employees of how these practices work and how their own pay is arrived at;

▌ provide training and guidance for managers and supervisory staff involved in decisions about pay and benefits;

▌ discuss and agree the equal pay policy with employees, trade unions and staff representatives where appropriate.

We intend through the above action to avoid unfair discrimination, to reward fully the skills, experience and potential of all staff and thereby to increase efficiency, productivity and competitiveness and enhance the organization's reputation and image.

Source: EOC Code of Practice on Equal Pay

Appendix 3

Factors creating pay gaps and remedial actions

Possible factors	Data required to identify factors	Possible remedial actions
Men and women on like work, work rated equivalent or work of equal value are paid differently.	1. An analysis of the average and individual rates of pay of all those on like work, work rated equivalent or work of equal value.	Investigate each case to establish whether or not there is a material factor such as differences in the performance of those concerned, market forces or red circling which might justify the inequality.
	2. An assessment of possible reasons for differences, eg traditional differentials, higher entry pay levels for certain categories of staff, market rate supplements, red or green circling and any of the other reasons set out below.	But a claim by an employer that a difference arose from different levels of performance or market forces would have to be objectively justified and red circling which favours any category could be regarded as discriminatory.
		If there is no material factor that demonstrably justifies the difference, the jobs in question should be compared by means of an analytical job evaluation scheme. If this indicates that the jobs are of equal value, steps would have to be taken to equalize pay.
Other measures of equal value, eg qualification levels, show pay inequalities between jobs in different occupational groups.	The use of a job evaluation scheme to establish whether the inequalities are caused by the systematic under-evaluation of one occupational group as against another.	As set out above.
Disproportionate distribution of men or women at the upper or lower part of a pay range or an incremental scale. This might result from the unequal impact of women's family responsibilities such as the effect of career interruptions because of maternity.	Distribution of men or women in the range or scale.	Review: 1. the length of the range or scale; if this is longer than is necessary to reflect the additional value that experience can bring to a role, this will discriminate against women and others who have less opportunity to obtain continuous experience; (2) the policy on fixing recruitment salaries (see below).
Men or women placed at higher points in the scale on appointment or promotion.	The most common point on the pay scale for the grade at which men or women are placed on appointment or promotion.	Ensure that policies and procedures that will prevent such discrimination are implemented. For example, produce guidelines that specify when staff can be recruited or promoted to higher points in the range or scale and emphasize the importance of adopting a non-discriminatory approach. Monitor such decisions to ensure that they are objectively justified and do not discriminate.

Possible factors	Data required to identify factors	Possible remedial actions
Men or women receive higher merit or performance pay awards or benefit more from accelerated increments.	The comparative level of merit or performance pay awards or the comparative incidence of the award of accelerated increments; the comparative distribution of performance ratings; the extent to which differences can be objectively justified.	Ensure that: ▮ men and women are equally entitled to participate in merit or performance pay schemes or to obtain accelerated increments; ▮ the criteria and processes used to determine merit or performance pay increases are not biased; ▮ managers are aware of the possibility of gender or race bias and are trained in how to avoid it; ▮ proposals for merit or performance pay or for accelerated increments are monitored to ensure that they are objectively justified and to detect and correct any bias.
Discriminatory use of a threshold merit bar, resulting in more men or women achieving a level of pay above the merit bar.	The proportion of men and women whose pay is above the threshold merit bar.	Review criteria for crossing the threshold or merit bar to ensure that they are not discriminatory. Monitor threshold or merit bar decisions to ensure that they have been objectively justified and are free of bias.
Market supplements applied differentially to men or women.	The comparative number of men and women receiving market supplements and their relative value.	Ensure that no supplements are awarded unless they have been objectively justified. Such justification to include evidence that the recruitment and retention of the staff concerned would be seriously prejudiced unless market rates were paid. It should use a number of information sources and should not rely solely on published survey material which could simply reproduce existing marketplace inequalities.
Red or green circling applied in a way that results in pay discrimination between men and women doing work of equal value or like work.	The incidence and duration and impact in terms of pay differentials of red or green circling for the different categories being compared.	Ensure that red or green circling does not unjustifiably favour either women or men.
Men or women in work of equal value or like work receive higher allowances.	The distribution and amount of allowances for the different categories being compared.	Equalize the distribution and amount of allowances.
A discriminating job evaluation scheme in terms of factors or weightings or the job evaluation scheme is applied in a discriminatory way.	Details of the factor plan and an analysis of the process of job evaluation followed by an assessment.	Revise the plan or the process to take account of any bias revealed by its assessment.

Appendix 4

Job evaluation scheme design: equal value considerations

Project phase	Checks and safeguards
Choosing the scheme	Select an analytical scheme or, if not, ensure that there is robust monitoring of equal pay – and that there is a process for comparing jobs across the organization, including one that will address 'equal worth' issues as well as 'like work' comparisons. If adopting a proprietary scheme, review factors and weighting for potential equal value issues; check whether the scheme has ever been challenged on equal pay grounds. Ensure that any external adviser to be used is knowledgeable about equal value issues.
Project planning	Select project team members on a representative basis. Select project leader that is sensitive to equal value issues. Train project team members in avoidance of discrimination. Build equal value checks into the project plan at every stage. Make implications of job evaluation clear to stakeholders – potential disruption of existing job relativities.
Defining the scheme factors	Ensure balanced selection of factors in terms of job mix and gender. Beware of potential to be influenced by existing situation and audience biases when collecting views about scheme and factor design. Avoid factors that are liable to indirect discrimination, eg length of service. Project group to review all test jobs on a factor-by-factor basis to highlight anomalies and inconsistencies. Undertake data review process free of any knowledge of potential points scores. Check for consistency of responses between men and women.
Analysing jobs	Ensure jobs are selected on a representative basis. Evaluator training to include equality and discrimination awareness. Involve managers and employees where possible. Be aware of potential for inconsistent interpretation in particular areas or by particular individuals.
Developing the scoring model	Do not use a single reference rank as basis for scoring model. Avoid changing weightings to address preconceptions about job rank order. Check weighting for potential bias – in relation to different types of job as well as gender.
Preparing for implementation	Pilot the scheme on an area which has many types and levels of staff; use it to finalize discrimination-free operation and maintenance procedures. Provide discrimination awareness training for those involved in ongoing administration of the scheme.

Appendix 5

Illustration of job stacking exercise

In this example, 25 cards have job titles written on them. Cards are first sorted into the 12 'largest' and 13 'smallest' jobs, then each of these groups is again split into a 'larger and smaller' group to make four groups. Starting on the left, the 'largest' job in each group is transferred into the next group, and so on until there are five groups of five cards of different 'sized' jobs, with the 'smallest' on the left and the 'largest' on the right. Use discussion of the criteria for moving jobs across to other groups to elicit factors.

Steps

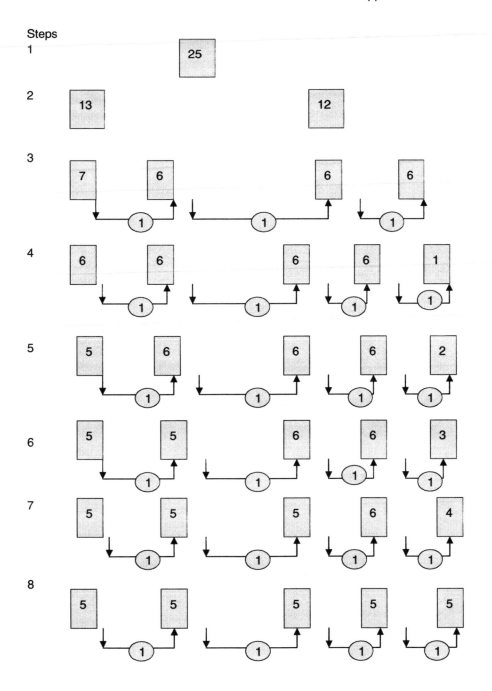

Appendix 6

Examples of job evaluation factors

Type of factor	Skills and behaviours	Responsibilities and effects
Skills and knowledge	Depth and breadth of knowledge/expertise Qualifications (minimum/typical) Applied expertise Technical skills Language skills Technical and industry knowledge Understanding of information systems/business data Manual dexterity	
Thinking challenges	Analytical skills Creativity/initiative/innovation Planning skills Problem-solving skills Strategic awareness	Authority to make decisions, recommendations or give advice Freedom to act/Autonomy/Latitude Consequence of decisions Strategic influence
Interpersonal	Communication skills Building relationships Influencing skills Caring skills Coaching/counselling/mentoring skills Team-building skills Leadership and management skills	Nature of people responsibilities Number of reports Impact on others, eg customer/client relationships Responsibility for establishing/maintaining different types of contacts, internal and external Requirement for participation in/leadership of teams
Resource responsibilities	Business acumen Financial awareness	Organization authority Financial responsibilities Asset management Accountability for/influence on delivering results International responsibilities
Impact		Size/timescale of impact on: ▌ internal operations; ▌ external reputation or perceptions; ▌ financial consequences; ▌ safety; ▌ company results.
Working conditions	Operational dexterity Physical effort Speed of response Need for concentration	Response to pressures, eg: ▌ deadlines; ▌ emotional demands; ▌ physical demands; ▌ speed of response; ▌ need for concentration; ▌ adaptability to influences outside own control.

Appendix 7a

Example role profile 1

Role title:		Department:
Purpose of role:		Reports to:
Deliver outcomes	**Required to:**	Expertise: Needs to have:
Develop others		
Build relationships		Focus of expertise:
Ideas and solutions		Focus of development:
Competency requirements:		
Other essential requirements for the role-holder:		

Appendix 7b

Example role profile 2

Role title:	Department:
Purpose of role:	Reports to:
Key responsibilities:	How are these measured?
Qualifications and experience required:	
Responsibility for resources:	
Technical competencies:	Behavioural competencies:
Other essential requirements for the role-holder:	

Appendix 8

AoC job evaluation scheme

BRIEFING NOTES

You will have been given a date and time for your evaluation meeting, which should last approximately one hour. Other than reading this document (including the attached list of the factors that form the basis of job evaluation) and then giving some thought to the points raised in it, there is no need to make any preparations for the meeting. The person who will 'facilitate' the evaluation will explain the process at the start and answer any questions you may have.

General introduction

The Gauge version of the new AoC job evaluation scheme is a fully computerized system that allows jobholders and line managers to be directly involved in the evaluation of jobs and avoids the need for any preliminary completion of job descriptions or questionnaires.

In effect, the system acts like a trained job evaluation panel, presenting a question about the job on the computer screen together with a set of possible answers. The holder of the job plus the line manager then jointly select the correct (or most appropriate) answer and the trained 'facilitator' will assist in this. The system will then interpret that answer and present a follow-up question to be answered. Different answers lead to different follow-up questions, allowing jobs of all types to be fully explored.

The questions will relate, in turn, to the 11 different 'factors' (or elements of a job) that have been selected and developed for the new AoC job evaluation scheme. These are listed on the attached sheet. Please think about how these might apply to the job to be evaluated, before the evaluation meeting.

Roles during the evaluation process

The facilitator:

- to explain the process to the participants and to operate the PC;

- to help participants to understand questions or answers;

- to help participants to agree the 'correct' answer if they initially disagree;

- to challenge any answer that seems to be inconsistent with other information;

- to ensure that the evaluation process is completed correctly.

The jobholder:

▌ to consider all aspects of the job, not just the more obvious ones;

▌ to answer questions as objectively and as accurately as possible;

▌ to provide examples of job demands, if requested, in support of any answer.

The line manager:

▌ to support the jobholder in considering all aspects of the job;

▌ to ensure that the personal attributes of the jobholder do not influence the answer selection unless the job has been formally redefined to take advantage of these attributes;

▌ to ensure that the selected answers reflect a proper balance between the job being evaluated and other related jobs.

Completing the evaluation

At the end of the evaluation the system will produce a narrative description of the job demands (the job overview), built from the answers that have been given. The jobholder and line manager will be asked to read this and check that it presents a fair, overall summary of the job demands – if it does not, there is a facility to return to any question and select a different answer. Once finalized, this Job Overview will form the agreed record of job content, from which the job score is determined.

Following the evaluation, the Job Overview and the scores given to the job will be examined and compared with other, similar jobs. If there appears to be any inconsistency, those involved in the evaluation may be asked to explain certain answers and, possibly, to amend them. This would produce a new Job Overview and may alter the job score.

AOC JOB EVALUATION SCHEME

The 11 evaluation factors and the focus of the questions asked when using Gauge are set out below.

1. Expertise

The first few questions will be to establish the depth of any theoretical/professional/ technical/practical knowledge required to do this job. (Note, the actual knowledge, experience, etc of the current jobholder will NOT, necessarily, be relevant.)

The next few questions will be about the breadth of knowledge required, including relevant organizational knowledge (ie of the College).

2. Thinking skills

The first few questions will be to find out how difficult it is to establish the nature and extent of the more complex issues or situations that the jobholder has to handle.

The next few questions will be to assess the difficulty the jobholder faces in deciding how to resolve the issues (or handle the situations) that the previous questions referred to.

3. Planning and development

The first few questions will be to establish the extent to which the development of new policies, strategies or curricula is a requirement of the job.

The next few questions will be to determine the planning skills required in the job and cover the nature, complexity and range of any forward planning.

4. Autonomy

The first few questions will be to determine the freedom given to the jobholder (within the College's, or other externally imposed, rules, protocols or procedures) to act on decisions reached without first seeking approval from elsewhere.

The next few questions will be to determine the breadth of impact of the decisions made by the jobholder, taking into account their diversity and complexity.

5. Communication and interpersonal skills

The first few questions will be to establish the content, range, complexity and nature of any subject matter that the jobholder has to communicate in doing this job.

The next few questions will be about the need for communication and inter-personal skills process during the jobholder's actual interaction with the other party (or parties) during the communication itself.

6. Responsibility for learners

The first few questions will be to determine any responsibility within the job for contributing to learning or skill development through teaching, assessment and moderation or other direct involvement in the teaching process or environment.

The next few questions will be to identify any specific responsibility within the job for the non-academic support or pastoral care of current learners.

7. Responsibility for staff

The first few questions will be to establish the extent of any responsibility for the jobholder to coordinate, supervise or manage the work of other College staff (full- or part-time) or contractors.

The next few questions will be to determine any responsibility in the job for the ongoing training or development of other staff, particularly staff outside the jobholder's line management responsibilities.

8. Responsibility for relationships with others

The first few questions will be to establish the range of the contacts required by the job with people other than College staff or learners.

The next few questions will be to establish the frequency of these contacts and their significance to the work of the College or institution, to the achievement of its objectives or to its standing or reputation.

9. Responsibility for resources

The first few questions will be to determine the nature and extent of any financial responsibility in the job, including income generation; budgets; expenditures; cheque- or cash-handling; etc.

The next few questions will be to determine the extent of any direct responsibility the jobholder has for non-financial, ie physical, resources.

10. Physical demands

The first few questions will be to determine the level of any 'practical skills' required to do the job (ie finger and manual dexterity, hand–eye coordination etc).

The next few questions will be to determine the type, amount, continuity and frequency of any physical effort required to do the job, recognizing any need for stamina as well as for strength.

11. Working environment

The first few questions will be to assess the mental demands placed on the jobholder by the job or by external circumstances.

The next few questions will be to find out whether or not the nature of the work or contacts with other people place particular 'emotional demands' on the jobholder.

The final few questions will be to establish whether there is any unpleasantness in the environment in which the jobholder is required to work or any unavoidable risk to personal safety and/or health.

Index